A VISIT WITH THE
TOMBOY BRIDE

HARRIET BACKUS & HER FRIENDS

BY DUANE A. SMITH

**WESTERN REFLECTIONS
PUBLISHING COMPANY**®

Montrose, Colorado

ISBN 1-890437-87-5

Library of Congress Control Number: 2003105227

Cover photo: The Tomboy in the 1970s. Courtesy: Duane A. Smith
Cover inset: Harriet Backus, c1907. Courtesy: Smith/Walton

Cover and text design by Laurie Goralka Design

First Edition
Printed in the United States of America

Western Reflections Publishing Company®
219 Main Street
Montrose, CO 81401
www.westernreflectionspub.com

7636097

TABLE OF CONTENTS

Dedicated to

a dear friend and historian, whose work I

greatly admire

David Lavendar

Preface

Upon hearing that Harriet Backus was writing her memoirs of the Tomboy days, a dear friend, Beth Batcheller, wrote her: "Good luck to you. You have done what I often thought of doing. I ought to write up our experiences. We have had them a plenty." Kate never accomplished that goal, but Harriet did in her book, *Tomboy Bride*.

Indeed, they both had enough experiences for several lifetimes at the Tomboy Mine, and, fortunately, Harriet persevered in her writing. To the delight of many thousands of readers, Harriet succeeded in having the manuscript published, although not without trials and tribulations.

I was fortunate to make Harriet's acquaintance in the 1970s and corresponded with her throughout the remainder of her life. What I gained from that correspondence about a wonderful woman, her grand marriage, her friends, and those "experiences" became the core of this volume. However, I highly recommend that *Tomboy Bride* be read before, or in conjunction with, this book. In her volume you will find the rest of the story beyond the Tomboy days down to her husband's death.

This has been a most gratifying and pleasurable trip for me into a vanished past. In Harriet Backus's day, the Colorado San Juans claimed the title of one of the country's premier mining districts. She lived there at the end of an era, and her correspondence and book opened for me a wonderful vista of times now gone.

Almost every author owes a great deal of gratitude to a host of people who helped along the way to publication. Obviously, without the assistance of Harriet Backus, her daughter, Harriet, and her grandson, Robert Walton, this manuscript would never have seen the light of day. The family tradition of helpfulness, enthusiasm, and love of history has been well preserved.

A generation of friends have jeeped with me to Savage Basin and the Tomboy, and on each trip I learned something new through someone else's eyes. A few of them became as scared as Harriet was when she first took the trail up from Telluride to the Tomboy, but they, like she, stayed the course.

Glen Crandall and John Ninnemann went there with me in the fall of 2002 and generously shared photographs they took of what remains at the site. As she has done for lo, these many years, my wife, Gay, not only visited the Tomboy numerous times but also aided me in various ways toward finishing this manuscript. While they did not realize it, perhaps, the rest of the family — Bucky, Tinkie, Cubby, Hershey, Thunder, and their canine sister, Toto — provided a host of fun and a few worrisome trips across the computer keyboard.

Duane A. Smith
January 2003

CHAPTER 1

Harriet Backus and Her Times

Harriet Fish Backus — teacher, wife, mother, and author — lived an adventuresome life in the first two decades of the twentieth century. In her splendid book, *Tomboy Bride,* she recounted her family's adventures from the Tomboy Mine, high in the Colorado San Juans above Telluride through Britannia Beach, British Columbia, to Elk City, Idaho, and back to Leadville, Colorado.

Harriet Backus had never been in the high mountains, but she came to love them. She could not "boil water at sea level, but learned to cook at 11,200 feet." She came from a genteel, educated background, yet she easily fit into the isolated, roughhewn, cosmopolitan life of twentieth century mining communities. While Harriet considered herself an "ugly duckling," she definitely was not. She did not consider herself a writer, yet she beautifully portrayed part of a vanishing America from a woman's perspective.

As she wrote, "I was late for my wedding," after traveling from Oakland, California, to Denver. That tardiness preceded a wonderful marriage that lasted fifty-eight years. While a Victorian woman in the true sense of the word, she was also a most "modern woman." She jokingly wrote me for example, "this caused considerable consternation in my family," about her traveling far away to her wedding. "Young girls like you," her father stated, "don't travel by themselves." Her mother did not mind that, "but it wouldn't be proper for her to be unchaperoned in Denver." She overcame such objections and went to marry her high school sweetheart. "Our honeymoon," as Harriet described it, lasted five days and cost a total of $77.60, including meals, at Denver's Savoy Hotel.

While *Tomboy Bride* provides fascinating glimpses into an era long gone, it, more than anything else, is the love story of Harriet and George.

Her love for George never died. When they were apart during his work, daily letters went back and forth, "his daily letter always reached me and my daily letter reached him." Of her husband she lovingly wrote, "I don't know of anything that was said against him or could have been said against him. It will be ten years in 1974 since he died and even writing this I can't keep the tears back." There were happy memories as well. "Yesterday [September 2] was my beloved husband's birthday and of course I relived much of our always happy years."

George had been a graduate of the University of California School of Mines and had entered the world of mining in Colorado. Before *Tomboy Bride* finishes, he'd worked at gold, copper, and molybdenum mines. In 1919, the family returned to Oakland and Harriet spent the rest of her life there with her beloved George until he died in 1964 after a long illness. The journey of the Tomboy Bride ended when Harriet died in August 1977.

My journey with Harriet began when I received a letter from her after reviewing her book for *Montana: the Magazine of Western History* in the Summer 1970 issue. A reviewer does not normally receive a letter from an author unless, perchance, the review had proved upsetting. That did not seem likely, in this case, as I had thoroughly enjoyed the book and only worried about the number of typographical errors that it contained. As the review stated,

This is a simple book, its virtue the homeyness and personality of the author. Pretending to be nothing but what it is, it succeeds, and Pruett Press should be congratulated for accepting it. Though minor points, perhaps, this reviewer does wish an index had been included and a sharper proofreader utilized.

As it turned out, Harriet agreed with my assessment, so I need not have opened her letter with "fear and trembling."

> *I repeat what I have said to my friends here and that is that your review pleased me more than the reviews written by quite a few newspaper reviewers and I quote the lines that especially pleased me. "This is a simple book . . . . Pretending to be nothing but what it is, it succeeds" and I thank you. The other subject is your remark about the proofreading and I thank you for that, too.*

Continuing with the September 30, 1970, letter, "So many mistakes in proofreading! One entire line was omitted in a dramatic event which happened at Britannia Beach." With her usual optimism, however, she ended, "I am sure they will correct many errors if I decide to have more printed. I have enjoyed my correspondence with them and know they, as well as I, will be happier when the most noticeable mistakes are corrected." She had great hopes for the second edition, later in February 1971.

> *In fact a second edition will be out in a few weeks and I hope with my red ink marking in many a page and with the help of your greatly appreciated statement that you wish there had been a "sharper proofreader utilized," this second edition will have been corrected.*

Those errors troubled her for years. Much to her relief, they were corrected.

In that same February her fourth letter arrived, and she explained why she wrote *Tomboy Bride*.

> *As I thought, I will probably never make a profit on the book but it has been and is still being a great adventure and I wanted to see the story of my beloved husband's mining experiences in print — in a good book form and I do think that the book itself is attractive and that the Pruett Press did a wonderful piece of work copying those pictures which were fifty to sixty years old.*

In April 1972 she sent a corrected copy to me with these sentiments.

> *The thought of them [errors] still bothers me. I am sending you one of the second printing in case you lend it to others, they would not think I could have made so many errors. I shall feel more comfortable to know you have a correct copy.*

A monetary profit would come, but money was probably the least of her rewards in writing the book. The renewal of old friendships, gaining new friends, telling people about the life of an earlier generation, and the joy of reliving the first years of her marriage, I believe, meant a lot more to Harriet.

Humbly, she did not describe herself as a writer. "Whenever any one calls me 'writer' I say I am not a writer but I have stories to tell. A real writer has much that a storyteller has not." She confided in an April 1972 letter, "I now look at my *one* donation of writing and wonder how I got through with it."

In the years that followed, we had a lively correspondence by mail and phone. I asked her numerous questions which she always graciously answered and, along the way, added a great deal more about her life as the "Tomboy Bride." She worried that she would overwhelm me with her "chatter" about her mining years. She never needed to fear that.

Harriet seemed like a member of our family. She never failed to ask about each of us and added a personal touch to her letters. A November 2, 1972, letter was addressed to our daughter.

> *Dear Lara: Thank you so much for the card you sent me. Your writing is very good. Please thank your Mother and Dad for signing the card, too. I am sure you will be a smart little student and you will soon know there is much to learn. This little kitten is saying "hello" to you. Your friend, Harriet F. Backus.*

The stationery had a drawing of a kitten and flowers on it.

Actually, I think both of us enjoyed our correspondence and both learned from it, certainly I more than she. In a June 18, 1975, letter Harriet commented,

> *How long it has been since I have written you! I have thought many times that I would enjoy receiving a letter from you asking questions about my living at the Tomboy. Yes, I enjoyed our correspondence very much.*

As the correspondence continued, she told a little more about her earlier life. In a September 3, 1970, letter, Harriet remarked,

> *Though I was financially unable to finish the University of California, I was majoring in history. I taught in a country school for two years. By that time my beloved husband was graduating as a mining engineer. I say was graduating because the class of 1906 was practically shaken out by the earthquake. He was on guard duty in the city [San Francisco] for the next fearful days.*

She enjoyed history. In a January 16, 1972, letter, while writing about her interest in the poetry of Alfred King, the San Juan miner blinded by an explosion, Harriet explained, "as I wrote before, history is of great interest to me. I am a saver of letters & papers."

A letter from her daughter, Harriet, after her mother's death, added more details to her family's story. Harriet Anna Fish was born in Oakland, February 24, 1885. With her brother and two sisters, she was raised in Oakland and attended school there. Born in Walla Walla, Washington, on September 2, 1883, George Stizel Backus grew up in Colville. "He inherited a small amount of money [his army father died in 1895] and decided to go to California to attend the Oakland High School, which had a fine reputation."

Harriet loved to tell about the first day George walked into her high school room. It was love at first sight on the part of both. They finished high school and both enrolled at the University of California, Berkeley, continuing the romance that started in high school.

Harriet's family did not have the "means to keep her in college," and much to her disappointment, her daughter wrote, she dropped out of college, "knowing she would be married as soon as possible, take a battery of examinations in San Francisco and earn a teacher's credential." Continuing on with her mother's story, Harriet explained:

For two years she taught school in Napa, California, while George finished college and received his degree in mining engineering. In December 1905, George was in the college infirmary with typhoid fever at the time of final exams and arranged to take them in May with spring finals. April 18, 1906, the San Francisco earthquake and fire (occurred). George went on guard duty in San Francisco for days, the University canceled all May finals, so George received his degree without taking any finals in his senior year.

Harriet, who did not keep a diary, wrote *Tomboy Bride* from memory, but her daughter said, "The stories are identical to those she told all her life."

Continuing with her mother's story and personality, Harriet gave the key to how she did it without notes or diary.

> *Harriet made up for her lack of a college diploma by studying, reading and taking courses all her life. They traveled a great deal on business and she always took advantage of her new environment by learning of its history and meeting its people. She was an extrovert. Her native intelligence was augmented by enthusiasm about everything, curiosity about "how and why," desire to learn, and a memory to retain what she learned. Harriet would ask opinions about geology, space, ecology, etc., of those she felt would know. Her memory was photographic. During her travels she never missed the chance to meet and talk to persons of all walks of life. A vast majority of those acquaintances became her friends. She corresponded regularly with new and old and it upset her when a "pen pal" was not heard from.*

I was now beginning to see how Harriet Backus retained and wrote *Tomboy Bride* with such zest and a clear memory.

One of the few firsthand glimpses we have of George come from several undated short notes he wrote to Harriet and his mother, briefly describing his duty during those terrible days in San Francisco following the fire.

> *Dear Harriet:*
> *"War is hell." But earthquakes and fire are worse. We are acting as guards in the city. Everything east of*

*Van Ness and So. of Market is burned. Thousands
are homeless. We do not know when we will be
through here, probably a week or more. You better
not attempt to write here but send mail to Berkeley.
We are on guard 4 hours and off 4 hours. Sleeping
on ground and our rations are 3 sandwitches [sic] a
day. We forage enough to keep us going.*

*Dear Mother:
I am on duty with VC in S.F. under commander
maintaining martial law. S.F. is almost entirely
burned. Savoy Hotel burned. I suppose Uncle went
to Presidio. There is no chance to locate him anyway.
I could not get to city before hotel burned. Marjorie
will have to do writing as I don't have time. We are
on guard 4 hrs & off 4. I am O.K.*

In a second note to Harriet he added,

*Patrolling S. F. Thousands have flocked to Berkeley
etc. I hope you are O.K. and can get provisions that
is more than they can here. No more college I understand. Lovingly yours, Geo.*

George was one of those men you rarely forget, and you
wished he'd been your friend. The younger Harriet described her
father as "a quiet, calm person of few words. An intelligent,
knowledgeable engineer." George, who worked for the Oliver
United Filter Company, later Dorr-Oliver, advanced steadily in
the firm. Appointed chief engineer in 1934, he eventually coordi-
nated foreign sales and manufacturing and served as "agents
coordinator," before retiring in 1953.

A co-worker said, at George's retirement, "you never objected
to accepting a tough assignment or where you were sent. You

always carried your smile wherever you went, no matter how rough the going was." Tomboy co-worker Alex Botkin, whose letters will be quoted later, praised George highly.

> *George was one of the finest men I have ever known. In his quiet way he could express convictions in a convincing manner but I cannot imagine his ever getting into a heated argument with anyone. He was genuinely liked by all.*

It is said that everybody has one good book in them to write, and Harriet Backus proved that observation. It did not come easily; she started writing in her forties and sent some pages to her Tomboy friends, the Batchellers. In a September 25, 1975, letter, Harriet explained:

> *I started to write my story years and years ago probably way back in the 1930s or so. I sent a few pages to him* [Jim Batcheller] *to see what he thought of them and if I had said anything interesting. You can see* [she sent along his letter] *that he had little to criticize but gave me very interesting accounts of the names of the ranges, etc. I stopped then doing any more work on my story.*

Despite working on it "once or twice" afterward, or that was how she described it anyway, it would not be until the 1960s, "more of less," that she really returned to the project and then only succeeded in getting the book published by paying for the first edition. She had a drawer full of rejection letters by that time, but true to her nature, Harriet never gave up her goal.

Many things interfered with her writing in the mining days. Travels with her husband on his work, USO work in World War II and after, George's illness, and the daily duties of a wife, mother, and neighbor took time away from her writing. Fortunately, she never gave up her dream and, despite her fears to the contrary, the effort proved worth it.

Tomboy Bride emerged a Colorado classic, which, more than a third of a century later, remains in print. Not, however, a classic in the sense that Mark Twain defined a classic: "A book which people praise and don't read." *Tomboy Bride* is definitely the type of book author Twain, in a less curmudgeonly frame of mind, had in mind in an earlier 1882 speech to a young audience: "There are many sorts of books, but good ones are the sort for the young to read. Remember that. They are a great, an inestimable, an unspeakable means of improvement." Twain was right and *Tomboy Bride* did that and more.

Young, middle-aged, and long-of-tooth, *Tomboy Bride* contains something for all ages. It captures and captivates readers about an era that now remains only in memory. More than that, it tells us a great deal about Harriet and George and a woman's role in the late Victorian era. After all, Harriet was born when Victoria was Queen of England, the horse and railroad reigned supreme, and telephone and electric lights were the newest inventions. When she died, a man had walked on the moon, television had reached almost every home, automobiles and airplanes reigned supreme, and major league baseball had crossed the North American continent.

While you, dear reader, might not think so, that last point is important. Harriet Backus was an ardent and devoted San Francisco Giants fan. When she found out that she was corresponding to an equally ardent and devoted Chicago Cubs fan, we had many delightful phone conversations and letter comments about the trials and tribulations of our two teams in the 1970s, a decade in which neither covered itself with championship laurels. I remember once when she became quite upset about reading that Giants players had been drinking on an airplane. That, she felt, offered a bad example to youngsters who followed the sport. We spent a long time on the phone discussing this and how times had changed. One thing about Harriet, when she called, it was like a local call, we covered a waterfront of topics. No worry that it was really a long distance call! The conversations were worth every penny.

Her comments over the years added spice to our correspondence. When the Dodgers whipped her beloved Giants, all she could only say was, "The Bad Dodgers!!!" Or, with her humor, "I am working hard for the Giants but do not have much success." On yet another occasion, rather than sitting down and answering a letter of mine, Harriet turned on the radio.

Yes, I would read it a little later in the afternoon for there was something else I wanted to do first! Can you believe it when I tell you I accomplished what I wanted to do? That was to sit on my davenport and help the San Francisco Giants beat the Houston team! And with Willie Mays' help I did!

She added, "I know little about the rules or strategy of the game, but I have pulled for the Giants ever since they came to San Francisco." She liked to refer to them as "My Giants." After the close of another season, with a fan's determination and optimism she predicted, "Wait until next year!!"

This reflects more than the mere pattering of two baseball fans. Harriet did not live in the past nor dwell on it. She had a vivid interest in the world around her — from baseball to changing life styles. Nor did she think solely about herself. A Giants' win was special, but so was achieving something else, "the knitting I was doing while listening was an afghan for our navy hospital." Into her eighties, she did volunteer work "at the USO and I can assure you it is most rewarding." Then she added a most revealing insight about herself. "I have done volunteer work for the service whenever needed really — even when my brother was in the Spanish American War [1898]."

She went to the USO on Saturdays, "my day there," and took a copy of her book to "show the pictures to the boys from Colorado, and of course they are interested." Harriet had a zest for life that shines through abundantly in both her book and her letters.

Tomboy Bride did much more than tell a story. It brought old friends back into her life and made new ones. On June 18, 1975, she wrote about her ninetieth birthday the previous February.

> *I was so pleased to receive a letter from a good friend of mine saying they were so glad I had written and published the "Tomboy Bride" because it has given me so much happiness in these last years. They are certainly right.*

With her usual honesty, she continued. "My memory of the past is still, I think I can say, 100%. What I forget are names of people and ordinary names of things." A good speller with excellent penmanship throughout her life, she fretted over their decline.

> *My handwriting is worse than it was and even spelling of words makes me think twice. You will excuse mistakes in writing and sometimes in spelling. So please excuse my ninety-year-old errors.*

Nothing stopped Harriet when it came to answering letters, however. She confessed "I received so many letters from strangers who are as excited about mining camps as I am, that I have them all filed. I hardly know where to begin." She enjoyed the letters thoroughly. "People I have never heard of have written from many of the western states. Some have lived in Telluride or nearby. Some recall the stories their parents have told."

Things piled up on her desk, much to her dismay. "I am glad your wife cannot see my desk. I am sure she is a fine housekeeper.

I have letters, articles, envelopes, et cetera piled high and am trying to dig down a little today."

Harriet always apologized for answering my letters at a pace she considered tardy, which it really was not. She seldom let anything slow her down, except health.

Apology, apology, apology! I wonder if I will ever get up on what I want to do! Whether or not I wrote you in October I do not know. As news spreads fast perhaps you have heard that I had a heart attack Nov. 5.

She lived at a Baptist retirement home in Oakland but to her, "religion for residents does not figure at all." With a chuckle she continued. "My church is the Unitarian's church and certainly they are not much alike." Her comment was so typical of the open-minded and tolerant woman she was, as she abundantly displayed in her book.

Harriet Backus was quite determined that her writing would not offend anyone, who might read *Tomboy Bride,* nor be a bad example for youth,. Therefore, rather than upset and embarrass them, Harriet declined to discuss topics that might offend her readers. For instance, pregnancy and a more controversial topic, the "red light" district, receive scant attention. In reality, she knew only a little about the latter and that undoubtedly was not a topic of conversation in the Backus household.

The Telluride and Tomboy world, to which Harriet Backus arrived, was not a frontier. That era had passed decades before and, in reality, had been only a blink of an eye before urbanization and industrialization replaced those overblown, romantically envisioned days of "pulp" history. *Tomboy Bride* refutes that image page after page. While it was not a world to which she had ever been, the mining west, in its own way, tried to emulate the various towns, states, and countries from which its people had migrated. The customs, traditions, attitudes, and even food had all mingled together. In their own interpretation, these folks upheld the Victorian world of their youth, a world that itself was fading.

Telluride had a population of 2,446 in 1900. It was the largest community in the San Juan mining district, itself world famous by this time. The Rio Grande South Railroad had reached Telluride a decade before, after climbing over Dallas Divide, back in 1890, on its way to Rico, Dolores, and eventually Durango.

The county seat, a booming economy, an opera house, a thriving school system, a hospital, a variety of churches, a "cracker jack" good baseball team, and a business district second to none on Colorado's Western Slope, Telluride had reached maturity in a most accepted way. A visitor could easily imagine themselves in an older, genteel midwestern or eastern town. Electricity, the telephone, and other "modern" conveniences had already reached the town and by the time Harriet arrived at the Tomboy Mine, the automobile had clanked and chugged its way into this mining district. The *San Miguel Examiner* (February 16, 1907) proudly proclaimed that the growth of Telluride telephone business had been "phenomenal during the past year." Three hundred ninety phones were already connected to the city exchange. Yes, everything was up-to-date in San Miguel's "metropolis" and its major mines made headlines with production and, unfortunately, labor violence.

Indeed, so "modern" had Telluride become that the *Examiner,* November 6, 1909, pointedly commented that the public school faculty "has been up in arms the past couple of weeks on account of the contagion of cigarette smoking by many grade school pupils." The school board intended to "stamp it out." The disgusted editor concluded, "the cigarette smoking habit which could and should be overcome" was not only affecting children but "men." Not finished, the article sounded a warning that has echoed down the decades. "The school is a splendid place to begin discipline," for the smoking habit "has never done anyone any good and will grow upon a person with age."

Visitors might have been shocked, or may have been intrigued by the red light district. Telluride also had a more wide-open lifestyle and remained a bit rougher around the edges than its mid-western or eastern counterpart. Shocking, too, was its early in the century socialist leanings as that political party did very well in local elections. The labor/management stress of the early twentieth century accounted for this deviation from the political norm. Neither the Republicans nor Democrats seemed responsive to labor problems. The good folks in the community still had a wee meas-ure of refining to do before Telluride measured up to middle class Victorian ideals.

Yet they could point with pride to their own orchestra, part of the Telluride Band. In March 1907, for instance, it was practicing new music for "Easter services" in the Methodist Church. It might have been a small orchestra in numbers, but it showed the aspirations of a community, and *The Examiner* expected a "most pleasing" service. Telluride was not called a "most progressive" town in many respects, but like its mining contemporaries, it was a town of contrasts.

Telluride was also the star of the mining district, the highest in elevation in the United States. Savage Basin, with its Japan and Tomboy Mines where George worked, ranges from 11,200 to 11,500 at the Tomboy site. The four greatest San Juan mines of Harriet's era — Tomboy, Smuggler-Union, Liberty Bell, and Camp Bird — were all set within a mountainous hike from each other. As everyone found out, they set at soaring elevations ranging from the Smuggler's 12,500 feet to a low of 11,200 feet at the Tomboy. These were not only major mines then, but represented four of the greatest in Colorado's and the West's mining history.

Three of these four mines had brought Telluride into its "glory" (the Camp Bird was in Ouray County, a fact Ouray never let Telluride forget) and kept it there after the labor troubles of 1903-04. Excerpts from the *San Miguel Examiner* stated: The Tomboy, Smuggler and Liberty Bell were "going along as usual" taking out ore that brought "up the dividends to a satisfying point for the com-panies owning them." Also "plenty of men all the time" worked there, producing an average "amount of mineral right along."

The headline in *The Examiner's* "Mines and Mills" column boldly expressed what locals thought, "Best Camp in the State." The March 7, 1908, column went on to proclaim it as "a field for investment that will come as near to bringing lucrative returns as any in the West." Without question, only Cripple Creek's production and wealth surpassed Telluride in Colorado in the years Harriet and George resided at the Tomboy. Very few precious metal districts in the whole West, either, could claim such production in the early 1900s.

The original claim that became the Tomboy Mine (initially spelled Tom Boy) dated from 1886, although claims eventually included in the property dated back to 1874. Failing to appreciate its golden worth, the claim passed through several owners. High in its basin, weather-hampered and isolated, development came slowly. Like the rest of the district, the turning point arrived when the railroad reached Telluride. Still the mine had troubles, the Tomboy Company could never seem to make it pay, and after reorganizing in 1894 with new owners and additional capital, expanded operations and placed it in more profitable production. They then did what many of their contemporaries did — put the property on the market. The well-known and respected veteran mining engineer, James D. Hague, inspected it in 1896 for the Exploration Company, a group of English investors.

By that time, it had a mill with a tramway to connect it to the mine, which they developed along the vein for more than 2,500 feet. Hague, caught in a November snow storm, remarked, "I have long since outgrown my fondness for snow," concluded his inspection and recommended, with reservation, the property be purchased. "In my opinion the mine will develop into a fine property but in its present condition the price is too high. It is a very good purchase at a reduced price, say $1,300,000 to $1,500,000." They wanted two million dollars. Transportation and winter problems caught his attention, but "work goes on without much regard to the season."

Negotiations continued as both sides dickered. Finally, in late January 1897, a deal was struck. The *Engineering and Mining Journal* (February 6) hailed the sale. "The fact that the English corporation has taken an interest in a Colorado mine is a good thing for the State, since it really means not only the full development of the mine in question, but further and probably large investments in other mines." Hague, who would become the company's president, brought the property in full and profitable production. Interestingly, the sale did herald British investment coming into Colorado, particularly in the San Juans and Cripple Creek districts.

The *Telluride Journal,* December 30, 1899, could not restrain itself, calling the Tomboy "One of the World's Great Gold Mines." Renamed the Tomboy Gold Mine Company (Ltd.), it slowly moved toward living up to that hype. Purchasing nearby claims expanded operations. A 1902 report noted it "should perhaps be classed first in this district as a dividend producer, but does not rank as high in point of tonnage."

In 1906, the initial year the Backus's lived there, the Tomboy topped one million dollars annual production for the first time. The mine would produce $22,000,000 from 1899 into 1924, when gold was twenty dollars and change per ounce. Of the four main mines, only the Camp Bird, in neighboring Ouray County, just over the mountain from the Tomboy, topped that amount in the same years. San Miguel County production, from the 1870s through 1923, totaled more than $70 million in gold, silver, copper, lead, and zinc. Ouray during the same period, produced nearly $78 million. The precious metals, gold and silver, however, accounted for the vast majority of that production.

Stockholders loved the Tomboy's production. The company paid nearly $2,200,000 in dividends from its purchase of the property through July 1907. Few mines in Colorado could match that longevity.

The company also used the profits rolling in to improve its mining operations and adopt some of the new industrial innovations. The *Engineering and Mining Journal* (March 23, 1907) reported the Tomboy was the first mine in the Telluride district to use electric locomotives. They replaced the "horse power used so long." That reduced hauling expense "considerably" and seemed "to work satisfactorily."

During George's days at the Tomboy, the company was having some metallurgical problems, which hurt mineral recovery and raised expenses. The concentrating plant, Wilfrey table, and the zinc plant were not getting "altogether satisfactory results." Separation of the iron and copper from the zinc worked, but a large percentage of silica remained in the zinc concentrates. As manager, David Herron, wrote this "has operated very materially against us in realizing the full value of the zinc ore." Such problems were not unusual in the mineral rich San Juans with its variety of base and precious metals. Zinc and copper particularly gave some mines and smelters headaches. The Tomboy eventually found the answers, but the Backuses had moved on by that time.

The Backuses lived at the Tomboy during the last good days of Telluride and the district. By 1910, the town's population had declined to 1,710. Corporation mining continued, while small-scale operations slowly shut down, their owners' dreams of riches gone. San Miguel County mining production, which stayed high until 1915 including eleven, one million plus years, dropped off after that before briefly reviving and then going into a long decline. Ahead lay more population decreases, World War I, the 1918 flu epidemic, and the "Roaring Twenties" which did not roar in the San Juans.

As Harriet recounts, the San Juans had just survived violent labor troubles in 1901 and again in 1903-04. The Western Federation of Miners fought the owners and companies as the reality of industrialization and corporation control came home to the miners. Once miners had been masters of their profession, now machines did much of what they once took pride in doing. Once they could "tramp" to a new mining district with tempting higher pay and prospects, but not anymore. Once they could "tramp down the mountain," strike out on their own, make a discovery, and become owners. That possibility had slipped away to nearly nothing. Once their skills had guaranteed employment; now emigrants, nearly fresh off the boat, took their places operating the machines.

Their pay had not kept pace with living expenses, and the profits rolling out of the mines went into corporate coffers and investors' pocketbooks. Despite electricity, hoists, power drills, and other innovations, mining remained the dangerous, physically hard job it had always been. Eventually no other choice remained except to become a laboring man in a highly impersonal world controlled by absentee owners.

The 1903-04 strike, one of the most furious and bitter in Colorado's history, shut down both of the major districts then operating, Cripple Creek and Telluride. With the backing of the courts, the governor, most of the state's newspapers, and the Colorado National Guard, the owners crushed the union. It cost hundreds of thousands of dollars, involved physical violence and death, violated civil rights, and left the state with a terrible anti-labor and reactionary image.

As bad as this was, it exemplified only part of a longer Colorado struggle, stretching from 1894 into 1914, between unreconstructed labor and its unions and the determined management in the hard rock and coal mining fields and towns. The two sides tore into each other with a vengeance in an unfair struggle. At stake was who controlled the destiny of the men and mines. Neither side thought much of the other. It had started in Cripple Creek, spread to Leadville, and eventually came to the San Juans. All of Colorado's major districts witnessed the turmoil. The last ten years were fought out in the coal fields.

It was not a pleasant time when George found his job at the Japan Mine nor when the young married couple arrived at the Tomboy. The union, for all practical purposes, was gone — its members blackballed and driven out of the district. The strike had benefited no one, crushed hopes, generated disillusionment, and left a strong anti-union stance among owners and their supporters. The defeated and driven out Western Federation left a hospital, which would play a role in the Backus story. The heritage of hate and mistrust would not quickly go away with the dawning of a new year.

Harriet and George were part of a larger story, Colorado's epic mining years. This era lasted from 1859 until World War I and created, settled, developed, and promoted Colorado. It laid the foundation for the state for generations ahead. They all came because of mining — people, towns, farms, ranches, railroads, industries, investments — and even tourists traveled there, as they said in the nineteenth century, to "see the elephant."

At this late date, it is hard to recapture the excitement, spunk, hardships, attitudes, joys and sorrows, and day to day living experiences that characterized this age, except through the writings its participants left behind, the newspapers they read, and the photographs they took.

It is interesting that women wrote three of the liveliest and most perceptive of all the first-hand accounts of Colorado mining. At a day and time when a genteel woman's place rested in the home, as wife and mother, they were not to be physically involved in mining. After all, some miners, the Cornish, in particular, believed it bad luck to even have a woman in a mine. They were not involved in the industry except marginally as wives and children. Amazingly, despite attitudes and realties, women produced three outstanding and highly readable accounts of these mining days. One describes the story of an ordinary miner's wife, another the remembrances of a childhood in a booming mining town, and the third, Harriet's story.

Anne Ellis, in her *Life of an Ordinary Woman,* recounts her poverty-laced youth as a miner's daughter, subsequent marriage to a miner who was killed in Cripple Creek, and her second marriage to yet another miner. She looks from the underside of life, in a sense, from a poor childhood to a not much better life as a miner's wife. In this bittersweet story, one learns of the trials, tribulations, and tragedies of her mining family, a typical one in so many respects, for the mining West, during the last decades of the nineteenth century and the first decade of the twentieth century. What was not typical was Anne, who persevered where a less strong woman would not have survived. She captured the joys and despairs, many more of the latter, in a way that collapsed any romantic thoughts regarding exciting adventure, or life, in the mining West of a century or so ago.

More joyful is Mabel Barbee Lee's *Cripple Creek Days,* which tells the story of her growing up in the booming mining town of Cripple Creek, Colorado, in the 1890s. Not that the Barbee family did not have its own shares of tribulations, they did. Her father, who "witched" mines much like people witch water with a forked stick, had his moments of success, but generally did not. What Mabel highlighted was life around her in Cripple Creek, at the time at its apex as a mining center and Colorado's last great mining boom town. She recounts that time with an enthusiasm that matches the era to a fair thee well. *Cripple Creek Days* includes memories about school, celebrations, fires, and the girls of the red light district. It is a peek at a world that is hard to imagine in our twentieth-first century.

Lastly, Harriet Backus, with her *Tomboy Bride,* fits beautifully into the trilogy of stories. Each looks from a different vantage point at mining and the way of life it generated. Mining, per se, is only lightly touched upon, except by Ellis and then from her tragic view. None of the three mined, although they did go underground to visit, but they related to and knew the world around them and preserved it in their writings. As a contemporary, the painter and sculptor Charles Russell wrote, in 1917, just as their books concluded, "The west is dead my friend, but writers hold the seed and what they saw will live and grow again to those who read."

Those who savor the history of Colorado and the larger mining West will find that these three authors offer wonderful, incisive places to start reading. Treasure their lives and linger several evenings then with these women as they recount their experiences. They will entertain, inform, and educate.

The pages that follow provide a potpourri of views into Harriet Backus's life and that of her friends at the Tomboy. They are not meant to replace *Tomboy Bride,* heaven forbid; they are simply to add and to supplement what she wrote.

Chapter 1 is meant as an overall explanation of how this book came into being and how I came to know Harriet Backus. Chapter 2 contains excerpts from letters she wrote to me. Over the years, I asked her many questions to help elaborate further on her life at the Tomboy. Her replies included much more than just that, she always graciously asked about my wife and daughter, discussed her family, and mentioned current events that had caught her attention. Those have been edited out unless they have a direct bearing on the Tomboy or illustrate Harriet's personality or marriage.

One thing that happened with the publication of *Tomboy Bride,* as she mentioned, was many of Harriet's long-lost friends got in contact with her again. It seemed that living at the Tomboy helped "guarantee" a long life into the 1970s. She generously shared the addresses of these people with me.

Excitedly, Harriet would write about a new contact. For instance in an October 4, 1974, letter she exclaimed,

> *Now I think I have found someone you will be pleased to write to. She has just read "Tomboy Bride" and is surely excited. Evidently her father was active in the San Juans. She surely knows about all that area and I greatly enjoyed talking to her.*

Another time she enthusiastically sent me a letter that she had received.

When I read the enclosed, I was quite excited reading that her father was the superintendent of the Liberty Bell in 1914. I thought perhaps she could give you some information about the Liberty Bell which might be useful for you.

Some of them, in turn, kindly shared remembrances of their lives at the Tomboy and Savage Basin. These are found in Chapter 3.

The photographic essay focuses entirely on the family and the Tomboy; Harriet generously sent many of these photographs from her collection. Other photos are from additional sources, and the latest show the site in 2002. While there was not much I could do to return her kindness and generosity, I did, on several occasions, jeep to the Tomboy and sent her photos of what it was like, and what remained, in the 1970s.

Among other items that Harriet Backus generously lent me were letters written at the time, but not to her. While not many, they are found in Chapter 4 providing further insights, particularly of the 1914 Telluride flood.

Chapter 5 describes Harriet's trials in writing the book. It also gives a real picture of the tenacity with which Harriet pursued getting her book published.

Chapter 6 provides a sampling of students' reactions to *Tomboy Bride*. They have been included to show the impact Harriet had on generations that came after her. I have used the book for nearly thirty years as required reading in my Colorado History course with literally only one or two students who did not like it. At the end of each term, they anonymously evaluate the books they were required to read. That is a remarkable record for an assigned book because, with a quiz up coming, such a book is not a student's most favorite reading material. Their comments about the book, as will be seen, were taken from the quizzes.

CHAPTER 2
The Tomboy Days Revisited

I savored my correspondence with Harriet Backus over the years and the enjoyment of knowing she could be easily imagined. She opened doors into her life, her days at the Tomboy Mine, and told so much about herself as a young woman and, when I knew her, a very active "senior citizen." I gained something from every letter or card she sent, while I could be little more than a friend who researched mining towns and mining history and relished discussing it with her. I did, as was mentioned, travel to Savage Basin on several occasions for Harriet and took photographs of what remained.

Her letters included so much more than the simple telling of those Tomboy days. This chapter focuses on those days, however, when Harriet, George, the Tomboy, Telluride, and Colorado were young and idealistic. You'll enjoy the occasional non-historic comments left in the letters, which give further insights into Harriet, the women, the wife, the lover of history, and the chronicler of a bygone age.

In a 1971 letter, just before the second printing appeared, she touchingly explained why she had written the book and why she continued on with new editions. She never forgot her San Juan days and her husband's mining experiences in those high mountains. It was not for profit she wrote, but her love of her marriage and those times at the Tomboy. It meant much to her and is worth repeating here.

*I expect the sale of "Tomboy Bride" will go much
more slowly than the first edition did but as they were*

*practically all gone I could not make up my mind to
have to say "It's out of print." As I thought, I will
probably never make a profit on the book but it has
been and is still being a great adventure and I wanted
to see the story of my beloved husband's mining experiences in print — in a good book form and I do think
that the book itself is attractive and that the Pruett
Press did a wonderful piece of work copying those
pictures which were fifty to sixty years old.*

The letters in the early 1970s came "fast and furious" as
Harriet answered my questions, remembered something, or contained a letter from an old friend, now re-found. A sample of one
is this September 25, 1971, letter. Her enthusiasm never wavered,
nor her excitement about discussing her Tomboy days and
George. In this letter she is answering a potpourri of questions I
sent earlier.

Dear Professor Smith:

*I enjoyed receiving your letter of Sept. 3 asking a few
questions about life at the Tomboy. Now we will
start with [question] #1 "Did you find the miners at
all religious?" Religion was seldom spoken of. One
incident still amuses me. It was on a special day.
There were no holidays at the mine, and the mill had
to be kept going. It might have been Easter. On such
days the company served the men a fine dinner and
invited the officials and wives of the few married
men. After the dinner we left the huge dining room
and visited for a short time in a small room. One of
the very gentle and educated men had a wife far from
attractive and apparently, rather uneducated.
Somehow the question of religion came up and two*

or three spoke of the churches they knew about.
When it came to this lady's time to speak up she said,
"I am an American."

[In a later letter she added this comment about this incident. "The others answered and I think, honestly, his or her
church which never reached our elevation (a variety of
churches) were mentioned.]

Now please excuse me when I tell you I still am
amused when I read your next question (Question
2). "When you had church at the Tomboy did a minister ride up or some local person conduct the service?" We never saw or heard of a minister go to the
mine. Mrs. Driscoll would gather five or six children
at the school house on Sunday and teach them some
little Sunday school songs.

There was no kind of amusement for the men. For
the miners it was work or sleep or occasionally rent
a horse and go to Telluride.

Finally the National YMCA approached the company which was very cooperative and said they
would build a building big enough for a bowling
alley. The National YMCA would furnish a small
organ and hymn books.

In "Tomboy Bride," Page 74 [page 85 in newer edi-
tions] I tell about the dedication of the YMCA, which
said proudly it was the highest chapter in the world.

Your 3rd question, "Did your husband get paid by
cash or check?"

My beloved husband was paid by check.

Question 4. "Do you remember how much of his monthly salary went for room and board for your family?" I wish I could remember what his monthly salary was but I cannot. It probably was very little — perhaps $125 or a little more. If in your record hunting you find the salaries of those years I would be interested in hearing about them. Of course, then we spoke more about wages than salaries. You say your *family. George and I were just the family until our daughter was born and a few months later we left there. We paid $5 a month for the teacher's little house. When we moved up the hill it was probably $7 a month for the shack. As to foods, you say* board. *We had nothing to do with the company's meals. We ordered our supplies by telephone. Going to the barn we used the telephone there. Our supplies came up on mule back and I remember we paid the mule company $1.50 for any load whether one load of canned goods or one little package. All our food was canned most of the year. We froze the meat immediately. We always figured on what we would need for a month so we would not have to pay too much [for] deliveries.*

Question 5. "Did you or anyone have a garden or flowers?" No, never. We had seven to eight feet of snow for months. Then when the middle of the year came there were always little batches of it and much truck[1] discarded and trampled [by] horses and mules and for a short time in the middle of the year the little donkeys came up with loads not as heavy as the mules carried. Only a short time did they work. The big elephant bloomed out in the summer with beau-

*tiful flowers (you please name these, I have forgot-
ten). The snow had fallen from the steep mountain
and there was nothing to interfere with flowers.*

*Your last question was "What was our most exciting
time while living there?" I had many exciting, pleasing times but I would say the most nerve wracking
time was when the electric wires crossed directly over
our house. I fainted, something I had never done
before or afterwards — pages 120-122 [pp. 134-136
in newer editions].*

Sometimes she took a little longer to reply, but Harriet never
overlooked my inquiries and each letter included an insight or
two into the *Tomboy Bride.*

Dear Professor Smith:
  [sometimes Harriet did not date her letters]

*Do you believe it is possible that I am beginning to
get caught up in the letters I have owed to "Tom,
Dick & Harry?" I want to fill in something about
those questions you asked me at the end of 1971.
First how did we vote? That made me laugh as I
really don't think any one there gave voting much
consideration. Of course there must have been many
in the canyons who were faithful voters but we were
so far from the political groups that we did not have
the interest. That sounds strange from me as my
father started me in taking an interest when I was
less than ten years old.*

*I started this letter yesterday and will try to have it in
the collection box soon. I have so much to say but I
am afraid I will not finish it today. If you could see*

my desk day after day piled high with letters I want to answer but I put off, put off, put off. It is strange but I am sure the fault is "old age."

Several of my friends are finding out that they feel as I do and that is we want to do things such as writing letters, going through my papers that I have had since and even before college days, scolding myself for not doing what I want to do. If you would just ring my apartment and enter I would wear you out with my stories telling about this life I have loved.

I am afraid the telephone visit from Whittier is the closest we can share. I certainly did enjoy it and from Harriet and Jimmie's letters they surely did too.

Now in this maze of papers I cannot find your letter asking about three questions. It is here. I had it last evening but no I can't find it now. So I will answer the questions I remember — now. I think my mind is working for I remember them now.

I answered the voting question. Now the church. In the first year or more church was almost an unknown word (not only at the Tomboy but also in Britannia and Elk City).

I have told this little incident hundreds of times. The few couples who lived at the mine were invited to dinner at the boarding house. I have forgotten the exact reason but I think it was Easter. Just about that time Mr. Herron had had workmen build a small building long enough for a bowling alley. The National YMCA had sent a tiny organ and song books. That was the highest YMCA in the world.

The man who went to have charge of it was a very capable and pleasant man. Not a minister but able to bring forth a little religion among the miners.

You asked about what we did in our evenings. There was nothing to do outside our little huts and some were working at night. So much of the year there were seven or more feet of snow on the ground that it was an effort to go out. Men worked hard, often under trying and dangerous conditions. As I have said and tried not to emphasize in what I wrote there were about ten or twelve women and only about four that had much in common.

With all best wishes,

Harriet F. Backus

The Batchellers were Harriet and George's dear friends both at the Tomboy and throughout their lives. They play a major role in *Tomboy Bride* and, as will be seen later, Jim provided the position, which took the Backus family from the Tomboy Mine. Harriet was real concerned in this letter about how she should address her letters. She never seemed to want to hurt anyone's feelings.

Dear Mr.)
Prof.)
Dr.)

Which one should I use? I have forgotten whether it was Mr. Keenan or Montana's splendid magazine[2] which called you doctor. Then I learned you are a professor; mister of course is proper. So you can see how puzzled I am.

I am sending you today some old, old letters from Jim Batcheller — and hope you can dig some small details from them and it is probably details you want.

Let me explain about the Batchellers. Yet I should not have to as long as you have read "Tomboy Bride." But I must tell you some things about them which of course I did not write about as I finished my story after we left mining camps.

Jim and Beth were two of the finest people I have ever known and I have never ceased about grieving over their early deaths. What wonderful parents they were and how they would have loved their grand and great grandchildren. Edgar, the baby in the baby buggy in Britannia Beach, is now Rear Admiral Batcheller of Washington, D.C. The next boy is a teacher of art in two fine private schools in New York City. The next one is now and has been for years the head of the ornamental horticulture department at U.C. Technical College at Pomona, California. The fourth has retired as a Lieutenant Commander in the Navy. He and Edgar both graduated from Annapolis. Edgar's middle son is a Major in the Marines having just recovered after two years of treatment for serious wounds as he led his men in battle in Vietnam and for that he received honors. They all call me their aunt. I am no relation but they have cherished the close companionship their parents had with my beloved husband and me.

Why I told you all this I don't exactly know but I have kept letters of our old friends all these years. I must add that after Jim gave up living in camps he took his family to Corvallis, Oregon, as he had been

offered the position of head of the mining depart-
ment at Oregon State. That building is now called
the "Batcheller Hall of Mining." The boys all keep
me posted about their families.

So I am starting sending you a little information you
might want. These pages from Jim I keep with all my
other possessions so when you have finished well
then I hope they will return safely to me. The old one
is hard to read. I have to use a magnifying glass to
get any of it but I know there are details in it which
I think will help.

Beth died in 1938 and Jim seven years later. I had
started my story but for years after I did nothing
with it. Only a few years ago I took up the writing
of it again. The bad Dodgers!!! [3]

Harriet F. Backus

As will be seen, Rob Walton, the two Harriet's grandson and
son, was very close to his grandmother. He helped her out on
occasion by answering my inquires. He has also been very helpful
to me in researching material for this book.

August 2nd '73

Professor Smith —

I arrived at my grandmother's yesterday as did your
letter. I've taken the initiative to ask her your ques-
tions, then take notes as she rambled on and on . . .
(she doesn't stop talking ever). I trust my writing this
letter won't lessen the import of the facts she recalls.

About taking care of her child (my mother), she says her first and greatest problem was that she didn't know how to care for a baby!!! Her husband was away after the birth, so she stayed in Telluride one month after the birth. The baby had persistent hiccups, and the nurse at the hospital often took the baby into the kitchen and sat in front of the stove to try to relax her. After returning to the Tomboy the nurse stayed 1 or 2 nights to get them settled. The baby had a bad eye soon and the mining doctor was consulted but was apparently not as experienced with pediatrics as with miners' injuries, but the eye problem eventually healed.

Grandma nursed my mother all the while they were at the Tomboy, and says she had to sit practically on the stove to keep warm at night. (The stoves were coal burning, with the coal brought up by mule.) The baby had colic every afternoon for quite awhile and Grandma had little success in quieting her, but the local (Tomboy) school teacher, Mrs. Tuller, was able to quiet her, and came over quite often after school. Grandma later found out that her milk was not rich enough, and my mother and uncle were slightly under nourished.

Grandma told me not to tell you, but she's very embarrassed about not remembering about the laundry — seems it's about the only thing she's no recollection of.

She remembers no superstitions about women in the mines.

She remembers Alex Botkin was one of few who played tennis on the dirt court below the shaft house.

She remembers no baseball team, and said no lodges were present. The holiday periods were not different from other days with the exception of presents brought by mail — they didn't go out much except to the Batchellers, apparently.

She did not go to town to attend a play, in fact remembers only 3 trips — to have my mother, to go to Denver, and one that she can't remember the purpose.

Concerning the union activity, she remembers stories of what happened before they arrived, the bombing of the Smuggler Union boss's residence, etc. but first hand, her husband apparently told her few unpleasantries, so she heard nothing about union trouble from him, but rumors reached her several times that trouble was coming — it never did.

That's about it for your questions. If you need this info in her own hand, she's quite well and could write herself, but I thought I'd save her the strain, and expedite the answers to you. One more interesting anecdote is that a doctor told her that the death of her 3rd child was quite possibly due to her diet — she had voluntarily stopped eating various items as requested by the gov't for wartime food rationing!!! She was too patriotic!

I enjoyed my trip to Telluride very much — took the jeep ride to the Tomboy, took pictures, and was greeted like a celebrity at the Miners Hospital where Mom was born. Grandma looks well, and like I said, is still talking. . .

Hope this helps —

Rob Walton[4]

Harriet wrote me in her next letter about Rob and continued to answer my numerous questions. She never once complained that I kept asking more!

Dear Professor Smith:

Your letter of July 31st was answered but not by me. That fine grandson and Harriet spent four days with me and I certainly enjoyed them.

I think the command of a first lieutenant in the Navy is still with Rob because the minute your letter came he said, "Now we will answer it right away." We were just finishing luncheon and he was ready to get the answers to you. I tried to tell him to let me think about the questions but no. I guess he knows what a procrastinator I am. He wanted to write you and so he started in, in his very nice way, to say, "Now, Gram, what special problems did you find in taking care of a family at the Tomboy?"

As to baby caring — I knew nothing about it and had had a month of wonderful care by Nurse Margaret Perril. Then it was up to me.

I think I covered most of this in my descriptions of Harriet's eye trouble and colic. I was weary about carrying her out for fear I would fall in the snow so George took her out when he came home. That nice Mrs. Watson who had eight children wanted to take Harriet to her home one day. I was a little weary but knew she would be carefully taken care of. So she was away from me for a few hours. When Mrs. Watson brought her back to me, she laughed and said she had given her a bite of food. I really don't remember what it was but I have always had a feeling it was jelly, in part. I worried and worried — what a dreadful thing to feed a nursing baby!! Then I would think that she had raised her seven remaining children and evidently fed them all.

What I even to this day think about is how she ever breathed in the nearly five hour trip when we left in that terrific storm. I had the blankets tight around her, and, as I said, I was afraid to let that freezing weather hit her face.

I add something here that I feel would not fit into a book.

When I reached the family home I took Harriet to a doctor who discovered right away that my milk had not been near rich enough and she had started on a "rickets" line. We were so happy that we had found it out in time (you were able to see that and caught it in time when you visited her in Whittier).

I think the only question you have asked me that I could not easily tell you is about washing. All I feel sure of was that clothes were not washed any more than necessary. I had an old fashioned washing tub that I put the clothes in on the stove. George would bring up the few extra gallons we were supposed to use. I would add snow to that and manage somehow to "do a wash."

Your next question was, "Did you ever run across any superstitions about women in mines?" No, I never heard of such a thing.

Yes, the tennis court was below our 2-room shack. I could look down on the court from that shack but not after we moved to the house on the tailings. It was seldom used and I think I am right when I say Alex Botkin was the best player there. A few tried to play with him but it did not last long, running at that altitude was "something!"

Some day I may get busy and tell you by tape a brief history of the Batcheller family that we have known. I could tell you that two finer people would be hard to find. I had for years the guest book she had at the Tomboy. There were the same names signed for the several (the assayer, electrician, mechanic) dinners she had. They left about three months after Billy died and we left almost six months after they did. I recently sent the guest book to their granddaughter.

You asked if there were any lodges. Oh, no, many had never heard of such things I am sure.

No, I never went to the opera in Telluride. I was in the town only a few times. Mrs. Herron invited me to visit her. I went [and] stayed overnight in their home — then started "up the hill" again. That day I saw the official of the Bank of Telluride, which handled the Tomboy business. Now this story I am telling you probably will come up in your research work. It of course happened several years after we left but we were particularly interested in it because we met both Mr. G. (I can't remember his name) and his wife.

I give you what I heard not what I know. As Telluride began to ail, people in the town of course began to fail and many left. Mr. G.[5] His Bank of Telluride finally folded in 1934 and, as she mentioned, he served jail time. [See Christian Buys, Historic Telluride (Ouray: Western Reflections, 1999), 258.] He went east and got a large sum of money evidently in the name of the bank. Then he proceeded to donate to the people whose work was failing. He was sent to prison in Georgia for years. Mrs. G. I understand waited for him in Salt Lake. That certainly must be in the records in Telluride.

George did not mention union activity. All that had happened in Telluride — but a rumor started once or twice at the mine. How I heard it I don't know. George would not speak of it for fear it would worry me. No unions were organized there.

Greetings to your family and you,

Harriet F. Backus

The following two letters, like the others, only include Harriet's responses to questions or fresh memories she remembered. She always included some family news or inquiries about my family. The thoughtful, kind, considerate woman of *Tomboy Bride* came through in every letter she wrote me.

October 21, 1970

Dear Dr. Smith,

Bulkeley Wells was manager of the Smuggler Union [Mine]. I spoke of him in my story. Unfortunately I misspelled his name as I always heard it as "Buckley" Wells. He was called "Buck." The legal

*battle between the Smuggler Union and the Liberty
Bell Mines started while we were at the Tomboy. Of
course, we never knew much about it then.* [6] [Federal
mining law gave the owner of the apex the right to
follow the vein beyond his claims sidelines. Lawyers
made fortunes off this controversial apex law simply
because in the nineteenth century it was hard to
prove the apex.]

*Now as to details Mr. Batcheller may have written to
his boys, I don't know whether they have anything
more than I have. After their mother & father died,
the boys went through their belongings and sent me
most of the pictures, papers, and letters which they
had about the Tomboy.*

Harriet F. Backus

October 19, 1973

*[Question about who lived at the Tomboy] One fam-
ily as I remember as the Fosters were there only a few
months of the year when their three children could
go to school. They left for the winter. The other few
huts were occupied by people with no children. They
seemed to stay by themselves as they did not mingle
with the officials (like Jim, Alex and Driscoll). Of
course there was always someone learning the mining work.*

*The miners' boarding house was quite a ways from
the tailings near which the cabins were built so we
very seldom saw the men except at a distance.*

That "all" is a big word when applied to the people living there. Besides about 275 single workers who lived in the boarding house there were about twelve couples married and living in the little houses or cabins.

[Writing at a later date — Mrs. Backus would start a letter, apparently put it aside then return to it a few days or week later.]

I said above about 12 couples in houses — the Batchellers, the Botkins (who left very soon), the young doctor Caplinger (they left after a very short time), the Driscolls (he had charge of the miners' meals), the Turners (he took Jim's place when the Batchellers left), the Matsons (who lost their baby), the Snyders (he started the highest Y.M.C.A. in the world) — notice that was its accepted reputation.

We had several nicknames for each other (now I am telling you some of our secrets.) For a while, and I do not remember how they started, he called me "Jess" and I called him "Joe" (not called just in our letters).

I remember you asked me once about the cemetery. I never saw it. I don't know whether or not it could be seen from the old rugged road.

Did I ever tell you about the stars? I never knew or dreamed there were so many. On a clear night I could hardly believe the countless stars — the sky almost filled with them.

Harriet F. Backus

Harriet over the years sent me a variety of material, all very meaningful to her. She never once hesitated about possible loss in the mails and excitedly told me to read this or that item.

June 19, 1974

Dear Professor Smith:

This note is to prepare you for receiving letters, pictures, clippings, etc., that I save — almost everything that refers to my years in mining camps.

One story I wanted to tell you was about ...three men — two on horses the other standing by [page 123, pg. 143 of newer editions]. The man to the left as you look at the picture was a company watchman. The man in the middle was the famous Bob Meldrum. [7]

I presume you have a copy of Tomboy Bride *so you can read on Pages 68 and 69 [pp. 78 and 79 in newer editions] about him and I will not take time to rewrite it as I want to add this story. The man standing and looking at the paper was a young Englishman. I didn't forget many names [that was definitely true, she never did discover his name], but somehow and why I did not admire him as I did the rough miners. I am hoping to get his name from Alex Botkin when I write him a note. That young man was the nephew as I remember of one of the English owners of the Tomboy Mine so you can realize the wealth behind this man. An English newspaper offered a prize to the one who could show the greatest distance in the world where that paper was read. The young man received a prize showing that the paper was read in faraway Colorado at an elevation of 11,500 feet.*

⤞ 44 ⤝

Now more of Meldrum. We left the Tomboy before Meldrum did, but we heard that he was in one of the northwestern states — I think, Montana. Still a sheriff, he was on the lookout for dramas. Something happened that caused him to shoot a young man, a part Indian that was liked by the people. This time Meldrum was convicted and sent to prison for how long I do not know. After a few years he got in touch with Alex and asked for help. Of course, Alex could not do anything for him. If this part of the story means anything to you, Alex could tell you more. I do so hope Alex is well for he remembers all the stages of his life and he is about 94 now. I saw him about 2-1/2 years ago and he was wonderfully "up and coming."

I enjoyed the short visit we had over the phone. I am surprised to think that I am still being asked for a copy of "Tomboy Bride." [Harriet always seemed amazed, definitely pleased however, that people wrote her about her book and/or asked her where it could be purchased.]

I am working hard for the Giants but do not have much success. [Harriet was right. The Giants ended the 1974 season in fifth place in the National League West Division. Those hated Dodgers won the National League pennant, but lost the World Series to Oakland.]

Harriet F. Backus   *Aug. 30, 1973*

Not all of her letters were long, sometime just a note about something that came to mind or an addition to an earlier question.

398 Euclid Ave.
Oakland, California
94610
Sept. 6, 1971

Dear Professor Smith:

I am enjoying the pictures of Savage Basin and pic-turing myself up there. May I be honest and tell on myself? Every once in a while I pick up my story and the thrill of it all starts immediately.

I say that now because I just reread your letter and you say that you think that Imogene Pass was not open when we were there. I really do not know though I have heard of it for a long time — I said George and I went over Virginia Pass. ⁸ I wrote one time years ago to the Telluride town office asking about the names of the passes. But what was meant by a pass? I think no point in the mountains was developed for travel, for few people ever went over the range. The little zigzag trail we took up to the top had been made so the two men who took care of Lake Ptarmigan, our only water supply, could reach the top and cross over any little openings they could find in the peaks. I would like to find out just where Imogene Pass is.

I am certainly glad you made the trip and I am sure you can be convinced that all I wrote is true even to details when you stop to think that the people, jeeps, the tourists seen now must be erased from the picture as it was in 1906.

Now just one more thing and I shall feel that I must never bore you again with so much chatter. This

*little addition is to tell you that Debbie Reynolds,
actress in the* Unsinkable Molly Brown *wrote me and
her mother wrote my daughter. They had tried hard
to find a copy of "Tomboy Bride" as of course she
[Molly Brown] was the wife of the owner of the
Little Johnny Mine in Leadville. Of course I knew all
about that as I lived there five years. I finally got a
book to her and heard soon from her mother saying
"Debbie and I read your book and the history is fab-
ulous. Wow! what an interesting life you lead — We
have been to what is left of the Tomboy Mine. In fact
part of* Molly Brown *was made [filmed] half way up
there. Oh what awful roads even now."*

*It was such a friendly letter I almost felt as though I
had known them.*

With all good wishes,

Harriet F. Backus

Some people fascinated Harriet, and me, and she often would
return to discuss them. I have included some of the comments,
which she referred to, from *Tomboy Bride* to further illustrate
those individuals.

Dear Professor Smith

*Please excuse my using this large business paper.
When I "rattle on" with quite a little to say this size
is easier. So here goes —*

(1) No, I never did see Mr. Bulkeley. [9] *In fact I doubt
if he was there while we were at the Tomboy. He*

probably had enough of the miners after they bombed his home. I think I sent you a copy of "My Association With a Glamorous Man — Buckeley Wells." It was sent to me by the daughter of Mr. Adams, the attorney for the Smugglers Union. If you have not read it, I will send it to you any time you want it.

(2) As to Mr. and Mrs. Herron — they were both charming. I never heard a word against either one. Mr. Herron [was] so very human and even though manager of a huge gold mine owned by an English company.

You might enjoy this little story, which I have always enjoyed though it is not for print. The office men wanted to show their appreciation for kindness to them by the ladies in Telluride and at the mine. George and I were invited. We sat at a long table in the boarding house. I was seated between Mr. Herron and I think the surveyor. There were about 24 at the table. The usual glass was above the plate. Mrs. Herron sat right across the table from her husband. The flunkies of the boarding house were waiters. The liquor, I suppose champagne, was poured and we started to eat. I never take liquor of any kind no matter where I am. The dinner was excellent. Mr. Herron soon finished his glassful then looked at mine. It of course was full. Luckily he switched his for mine. Then he called the flunkie, "Keep Mrs. Backus' glass full," he said. Sam the surveyor's glass was empty so he switched glasses with mine. Those who sat near saw what was happening and began to laugh. Mrs. Herron said, "Davey, don't do that." All those toward this end of the table didn't see why they were laughing but some noticed my glass was filled quickly. I must say that with all that nonsense the entire dinner and evening were dignified and delight-ful. None of the officials were drinking men and as no liquor was allowed at the mine except for a spe-cial occasion we never had trouble. However three days later the rumor spread that I drank more than anyone else at the table.

Mr. and Mrs. Herron were devoted parents and raised their children excellently. In "Tomboy Bride" Page 71-72 [pp. 81-82 in newer editions], I told about how the Herrons used water in the time they spent at the mines in Nevada before going to Telluride. [When we lived in Nevada where David was mining, we had to buy water by the bucket at a high price and bath night for one had to be bath night for the entire family. We had a round galvanized tub in which we washed the baby first. Then in the same water, turn by turn, went the next oldest child until all four were bathed. Afterwards, I took my turn. David came last, scrub-bing the grime from his mine-soiled body with that well-used water.] She was surely a "good sport." After we left the Tomboy Mr. Herron asked George to watch for a good prospect so we heard from him for several years. They moved to Los Angeles and I think he died comparatively young.

(3) You asked about Meldrum. I think the bottom of Page 68 [pg. 78 in newer editions] described him as well as I can. [For years a deputy sheriff, Meldrum was said to have killed more than a half score of men as an officer of the law . . . . Of medium size, with a swarthy skin, black hair, and heavy moustache, Meldrum looked like the typical intrepid westerner . . . . He rarely spoke to anyone, perhaps

because of extreme deafness, but what he lacked in hearing was made up in keen vision.]

Now right here I will tell you about Alex Botkin who figures in the first part of my story. I will give you Alex's address. You might want to write and ask him some questions. In June he could still tell about everything when he was at the Tomboy. (You can see that my scribble is getting worse.)

[original # four deleted — an address]

(4) No, no miners in particular stand out in my mind. I will enclose a paper Jim sent George years and years ago with pictures which I think are typical. I may have told you about the one thing I feel I can justify in complimenting myself about. That is that it did not take me long to learn that a miner's language is not what I was used to and that I had sense enough to ignore it. I was always treated with courtesy. One of the Batcheller boys told me his mother and little Billy were in the front of their cabin in deep snow, the mule train right near them was having trouble as one mule was having trouble. The muleskinner asked Beth to take Billy and go into their house as he didn't want them to know what he was going to say to his mule, probably beating him with a shovel at the same time.

(5) You asked if George talked about life in the mines. No, because he was very seldom in the mines. His work all his life was the machinery part of all his work. Several times when we were in Leadville he had to go to mining claims to examine the veins. The six weeks we were in Butte, where he worked about 2,000 feet under-

ground, and a few other examinations of claims were the only times he was underground.

(6) My opinion of Telluride — I was in Telluride so seldom that it is more or less like a picture to me. I have a dim feeling that I stayed over night with Mrs. Herron when I went down, probably to see the doctor. I was there quite a while before Harriet was born. I will say here, women then were very different from women now. A pregnant woman worked hard to hide her shape. Mother sent me a dress long before it was time for our baby. It fell straight down from the shoulders, very full so as to hide the form. When I was taken down to Telluride, I stayed in my room most of the time so my condition would not be noticed. Here's another note not for print. [I had written to Mrs. Backus about the possibility some day of compiling her letters and other things into a book.]

Harriet was due in August but she passed by that month. George's birthday was September 2nd and I thought it would be fine if I could give George a living birthday present. So a couple of days before September 2nd I started to walk up the steep paths nearby. It happened that our doctor was in that area and asked me what I was climbing like that for. My answer was I wanted the baby to come on the second, but she didn't. She picked out September 9th. She must have known she would spend most of her life in California whose birthday is 1850 — September 9. [10]

The nearest I came to seeing any other mine was when we rode over the pass and I saw the boarding house and mill (did not go through it) of the Camp Bird. By the way did you ever read Father Struck it Rich *by Evelyn Walsh McLean? It is interesting but I did not like her character and never thought she wrote the book entirely by herself. Her father made millions out of the mine, and she ended up as a star in Washington entertaining the government's outstanding men.*

(7) The only thing I knew about the red-light district was it was on the road from Telluride to Pandora and that the miners rented horses for a day or so and probably went there riding the poor horses so fast to get back to work that often a horse was wind broken and unable to climb up the trail again. Of course that was the understanding among some. [11]

Harriet F. Backus

She generally referred to me as "professor," although occasionally used Duane and in the letters always called my daughter and wife by their first names.

October 9, 1973

Dear Professor Smith

How I wish that I had the energy to write my friends and relatives as I did not long ago.

I want to write to many whom I continually think about but I don't have much luck. I try to argue with myself but even that does not help.

So please excuse these scribbled notes for I do enjoy so very much feeling that my details of part of my happy life are being worked into what a splendid history I am sure your book will turn out to be.

You asked about the school house. It was just one large room and school was held only for five months. Sunday School there, too, as there was no church.

One little family lived at the "Upper Working." I have forgotten their name as I saw them only a few times. They had one little boy who was somewhat lame though there was hope that he would improve. We were told that his loving father was tossing him over his shoulders when the boy was very young and unfortunately the child's leg was hurt. They were very nice people and we felt sorry for them. I remember all the people who were there when we were — note the date in the above. This is over a week later and looking it over I see several poorly worded sentences.

Harriet F. Backus

The Tomboy days became a memory for Harriet when George received this letter from their friend Jim Batcheller. George accepted, the family moved, and her recollections mellowed into interesting stories and memories, which she recounted in *Tomboy Bride*.

October 28, 1910

Dear George,

Would you accept position here as assayer, to begin with $125.00 per month, — board $1.00 per day, Hospital $1.50 per month. Nice little house goes *with the position, Rent $5.00 per month — Running water in house — at present Co. does not charge for electric lights.*

Of course you understand that there are what may be called mining chances but I believe unless copper drops to nothing, this job will last. Furthermore I believe it will better, and has sufficient prospects to be worth your while to try. I know from what you have said you do not look at assaying as a permanent professional job. You will have a pretty fair equipment here, with two pretty well trained [individuals?] for sample men, to cut down, dry, and buck samples and do most all of the rough labor. At present there is also a Golden (Colo.) under grad here as an assistant — but this arrangement may not be permanent.

Please wire me my expense
c/o Britannia Mining & Smelting Co.
Foote's Parcel Dispatch
Vancouver — B.C.
if you will accept — also how soon you can get here.

If you want to move your family up you can take the time all right and they will be looked out for until you can move into your house — Board $1.00 per day would only apply if you come up alone.

All I would like is to have you come as soon as you conveniently can.

This offer is something new that has come up very recently and is immediate, and separate from the shift boss matter I wrote you of.

I will follow this with more details of how to reach here. If you accept don't wait for further word but pack up and start.

Good Luck to you

"Batch"

The rest of their adventures, until finally settling in Oakland, California, are recounted in *Tomboy Bride.*

---

[1] Mrs. Backus is referring here to rubbish.

[2] Jerry Keenan was the editor for Pruett that worked with Mrs. Backus on her manuscript. She is referring to my review which appeared in the *Montana Magazine* and an article I wrote in the Summer 1970 issue.

[3] For the non-baseball readers, the Brooklyn Dodgers, later the Los Angeles Dodgers, were the "mortal" enemies of Harriet's Giants. Over the years, there have been some classic games between these two teams. The Dodgers did not seem to be on Harriet's favorite list!

[4] Rob Walton was very helpful in adding information, photographs, and other material, which greatly enhanced the story. After his mother's death, he inherited all his grandmother's records.

[5] Telluride banker, Charles Waggoner was the individual Mrs. Backus referred to in her letter.

[6] Bulkeley Wells became a contentious figure in the labor/management conflicts as shall be explained in a later chapter. The Smuggler-Union and Liberty Bell lay in adjoining basins separated by mountains. It turned out to be a nasty squabble over trespass and ore removed from the Smuggler. The Liberty Bell lost the judgment and appeal and paid over $400,000 in damages. Errors in surveying and the question of where the vein apexed (highest point) led to the trouble.

[7] Mrs. Backus is referring to the first edition of *Tomboy Bride* (1968). "Professional gunman," Bob Meldrum was nearly deaf which made him doubly quick to take action. He was hired by the mine owners during the strike to keep the "peace." When the troubles quieted down, Meldrum eventually drifted on to other places where his services might be needed. He was ultimately found guilty of killing a cowboy in Wyoming (1910) and served his "punishment" working for ranchers in the Rawlins region. See Gene Gressley, *Bostonian and Bullion: The Journal of Robert Livermore 1892-1914* (Lincoln: University of Nebraska Press, 1968), pp. 97-99.

[8] The USGS maps and other maps in the author's files do not list a Virginia Pass for the Tomboy area.

[9] Bulkeley Wells was the point man for the owners during the 1903-04 strike. His uncompromising position led to repeated trouble with the "union trouble makers agitators" particularly because Capt. Wells commanded the Colorado National Guard unit during the strike.

Colorado governor James Peabody enthusiastically aided the owners here and at Cripple Creek. Harvard graduate, mining engineer, Wells managed the Smuggler-Union Mine and was quite a socialite. See Buys, *Telluride*, Gene Gressley (ed.), *Bostonians and Bullion,* and Martin G. Wenger, *Recollections of Telluride Colorado: 1895-1920* (Durango: Privately Printed, 1989 reprint).

[10] California was admitted into the Union on that date as part of the Compromise of 1850. The slavery issue had previously created a long and bitter debate because of the proposed free-state constitution.

[11] Being a proper Victorian woman, Mrs. Backus would not have discussed the Red Light District and no doubt her husband George would have shielded her from this as he did other things. The district along East Pacific Avenue contained parlor houses, cribs, gambling halls, and saloons. She probably never visited that part of town or any other where such activities went on, although she obviously knew of them.

CHAPTER 3
Friends:
Their Experiences at the
Tomboy and Telluride

The following letters are from Harriet Backus's friends to me. Each in its own way contributes to the varied story of the Tomboy Mine, Telluride, and life in the San Juans just after the turn-of-the-century.

The letters have been slightly edited to exclude any personal material that does not contribute to telling an earlier story. Some repetition will be found, yet, it leads into other bits of news, so no harm was done by leaving all the reminiscences together.

Alex Botkin, first introduced in *Tomboy Bride,* shares some of his experiences as part of the Company management. A close friend of the Backus family, his letters focus on his life at the Tomboy. Mildred Ekman was a child at the mine, so her view is somewhat different. Martha Gibbs recalls the years that Harriet Backus journeyed to and from and briefly stayed (awaiting her first baby's arrival in Telluride). Jim Batcheller's comments were originally sent to Harriet.

Alex Botkin worked at the mine with George. He and his wife became close friends of the Backuses and shared moments with them as Harriet recounts in *Tomboy Bride.* Alex gives a different perspective of the Tomboy operation.

Maryville Nursing Home
14645 S. W. Farmington Road
Beaverton, Oregon

Nov. 7th, 1972

Your letter just arrived and I will answer it as well as I can. As I am ninety-seven years old you will understand that my memory may not prove too good. I had been working for the Northern Pacific Railroad in St. Paul as clerk for the Asst. Gen. Supt. in charge of the eastern divisions at a salary of $100 a month. I was engaged to my wife-to-be when I received a letter from an old Helena, Mont. friend saying I could get a job at the Tomboy Mine near Telluride, at a salary of $150 a month. My wife-to-be urged me to take it so we could get married sooner.

My education in college consisted of three years at the Sheffield Sci. School of Yale. [1] *I would have taken a course in mining engineering, but they had none so I majored in chemistry, but have never had any use for it. I worked at the Tomboy a year before returning to St. Paul to get married.*

My work at the Tomboy was merely that of a clerk at the mine office so I have never had any real mining experience. But my wife and I lived in a log cabin for over four years and it was to say the least a unique experience, and interesting.

Of course in my position I got to know the mine and mill and other members of the staff. And as I delivered the checks to the mine workers I got to know quite a few of them intimately. And as Mrs. Backus told you

I knew Bob Meldrum. But let me say now and confidentially that I personally had a different feeling about him, than even the Supt. My personal feeling was that as a Deputy Sheriff and guard at the mine he was disliked by the miners who more or less resented having a sort of detective on their heels all the time.

There are many stories about friends I made at the mine I could tell you but comparisons could well be unfair and I would hate to praise one at the expense of another, especially in writing. For example I had enormous respect for Mr. and Mrs. George Backus, a very courageous and highly practical young couple. When the Japan Mine below the Tomboy closed down, he [George] readily found employment at the Tomboy, and I know Supt. Herron thought a great deal of him. In any mishap where he worked, he had the knack of doing the important thing for the moment and let investigations for its cause wait.

You asked me who, among employees, stand out in my mind most. Of course they would be the mine and mill foremen and the rest of the staff. I will now list them. Mine Foreman, John Spargo, self-educated but a miner of great experience. Mill Foreman, Jim Batcheller, graduate of M.I.T. Wife with him at Tomboy. [2] *Electrician, Don McKeehan, single and I believe had college. Master Mechanic, Al Awkerman, self-educated, a genius in mechanical repair and upkeep. Assayer, Leslie Barnett, nephew of the London man in charge of Tomboy. He was killed in the World War [WWI]. Doctor, Dr. Edgar Hadley with offices at the mine and at Telluride. My personal assistant, Krammer, who attended to matters when I was at home with my wife.*

All these I have mentioned had one thing in common. They were gentlemen, and my wife frequently would invite one or more for dinner and an evening together.

Sincerely yours,

A. W. Botkin

In his next letter, we find out that Alex played on the Tomboy baseball team and experienced some different things from George and Harriet Backus.

Nov. 29th, 1972

Dear Sir,

I have your letter of the 24th and first of all will answer your questions as well as I can.

My duties as clerk at the Tomboy consisted in keeping track of supplies needed and kept in a storeroom in the basement below my office, issuing them out on requisition and sending to the Telluride office each month a list of any needed material.

Each day amalgam balls[3] would be brought to my office from the mill and placed in a vault until there was sufficient amount for the next process of removing as much mercury as possible, leaving the crude gold as we called it, and this in turn being melted down and made into bars of gold, each about the size of a brick. I had to weigh and make a record for the Telluride office. And when the bars of gold were taken to the bank in Telluride I had to take a small

*sample from each bar for our assayer at the mine to
determine the fineness. The bars were taken to
Telluride on the back of a mule with a heavy chain
around his belly, the key for opening it being in the
hands of the bank only.*[4]

*The daily trips of mule trains, fifteen mules each, took
supplies to the mine and brought back the concentrates for shipment to the smelter.* [5] *I would report all
these and time of departure of the mule train taking
the bars down to the Telluride office. This about cov-
ers my duties as clerk except some simpler matters
such as collecting rents and delivering pay checks to
the miners, these having been made up at the Telluride
office. Yes, I was the Botkin mentioned in the Telluride
paper playing on the ball team and at tennis. I cannot
remember any baseball field* [6] *at the Tomboy and that
one game was the only one we ever played and that
was not in Telluride but on our opponent's field, the
infield of which was fairly level but the outfield had
many tree stumps sticking up.*

[The *San Miguel Examiner,* Saturday, June 6, 1908, reported that
a "bunch of ball players came down from the Tomboy Thursday
afternoon and played the Telluride team on the home ground.
Previous to that time the town boys had expressed a desire to play
them a match and they accepted so quickly that no time was given
for public notice and many a fan is regretting the fact that they
were [not] on to it so he could see the game." Baseball was always
a popular sport in the mining communities (playing, watching
and gambling on the outcome), so their disappointment is understandable. The weather "was decidedly inclement with the wind
something fierce." Still, "about 250 turned out" to see "Telluride
win 16 to 4 in seven innings. Alex Botkin played shortstop and
led off for the Tomboy team."]

*I was at the Tomboy a year before getting a layoff
and returning to St. Paul to get married and I married in 1905. Altogether I was at the Tomboy for
about five years, four after being married. A cousin
of my wife, a well to do widow, was very much upset
at her spending any more of her life at that terrific
elevation and wrote her a letter asking her to get me
to resign and take her back into civilization. When
the letter came to my office, not knowing its contents
I sent it to my wife by my Great Dane dog [Thyra].
But after he left the office with the letter in his mouth
I began to wonder why my wife should be hearing
from her at this time of year. So I left the office in
charge of my helper and went home to see what the
letter had to say. On reaching our cabin I called out
to my wife and in a crying voice she called out, come
quick. I asked her if she had had any bad news from
her cousin. Read this, she said and handed me the
letter. It was the request that I resign at once but
added that she realized I would have to find other
employment and we would be under considerable
expense so was sending a check to help us through.
That dog had carried home a letter with a check for
five thousand dollars. Needless to say I did resign,
and eventually we bought some land near Estcada,
Ore. and starting to raise apples first, prunes second
and some ginseng and Golden Seal. But this is not
Tomboy material.*

*There are many stories of life at the Tomboy I could
give. The Tomboy had gone through a very difficult
period with labor troubles before I was there and of
course I heard some of that. For example when the
trouble at the Tomboy was at its height the governor
(I think it was Peabody)* [7] *sent a man to Telluride to*

look into the trouble and report to him at once if
troops might be necessary to bring about peace and
the closed mine reopened. He may have been a member of the legislature. His reply to the governor was
famous. I cannot be sure of exact wording but in
affect it was "Troops unnecessary, miners in peaceful
possession of the property." Although of course they
did not own a single share of stock.

Telluride[8] was a small mining town with some delightful people but of course with the underworld well represented. There was a dance hall where both private
and public dances were held. Mr. Herron,[9] Tomboy
Supt., thought it would be nice to have a party at the
Tomboy for the friends in Telluride. The dining room
at the Tomboy was made into a dance hall for that one
evening. Wives of the staff did a wonderful job with
wild flower decorations. To be sure we would not
have more hosts than guests we drew the line at shift
bosses. [Not knowing how many were invited to this
dinner, it is hard to make a judgment on this decision.
There were however numerous staff, from the general
manager through the shift bosses, at this large mine
and it is understandable a line had to be drawn some-
where.] Next morning there appeared at my office the
wife of a shift boss, very elaborately dressed. I said
"Good morning, Mrs. _____, did you want to see
me about something?" "I want to know why the shift
bosses and their wives were not invited to the dance."
I explained as I have already written whereupon she
added "Well Mr. Botkin, let me tell you that where
Henry and me come from we were used to going with
the best." [It would seem that she and Henry felt they
could more than hold their own amid the company
"elite." It was not unusual to have some tension,

particularly socially between the various management groups who came from different backgrounds, education levels, cultural heritage, and experience.]

I considered my life at the Tomboy very interesting but of course there were occasional trying moments, due almost always to misunderstandings. When I took the job I was told by the Supt. himself that my immediate boss would be Mr. Tobin,[10] in charge of the Telluride office, and that he would give instruction which should be followed. But in doing just that, I occasionally found myself in some difficulty because such instruction in some manner was contrary to the Superintendent's wishes. In short, I encountered some difficulty with two masters. [Botkin was caught between the mine staff at the Tomboy and the company's Telluride staff. It was not inconceivable that they sometimes worked at cross-purposes.]

The typewriter I am using is a very old one but I should not blame it for my poor typing. At 97 years I am not as good a typer as I used to be.

I am sorry to hear of Mrs. Backus heart attack but hope she is fully over that. I must write her. She deserves much credit for her "Tomboy Bride" and I trust her family fully appreciates the amount of work she put into it.

Now just one other thought before I close. Of course in my position I knew Bob Meldrum.[11] But (personally), although I admired his courage and daring, also know from miners I knew well that they resented being more or less heeled [followed closely or checked on] by a detective. For example, Mr. Herron, Bob and I were in my office on the Tomboy property. Mr. Herron casually remarked, "I wonder what those miners are up to tonight." Instantly Bob rose to his feet and starting to leave and said, "I'll go over and see." Of course Mr. Herron stopped him at once. The last I heard of Bob he was serving a life sentence in Wyoming for having killed a half breed Indian. It was during those feuds between cattle and sheep owners in Wyoming.

Sincerely,

A. W. Botkin

Mt. Botkin wrote again:

December 27, 1972

First let me answer your questions as best I can. Yes, I remember the Y.M.C.A.[12] but it did not last as long as intended. Next to their headquarters was a bowling alley built by the management and much appreciated by the miners and mill men. It was a nice change from the usual source of amusement, gambling at the store. But there came some rumors of discontent from the miners in time and the management, after making a careful investigation, decided that there was good reason for the miners' complaints and that was the end of the Y.M.C.A. I do not know just what the nature of their complaints was. [Considering there were various shifts working at the Tomboy, the hours the "Y" was open might have been a problem. Probably, the management stopped gambling, a favorite pastime, prohibited swearing, and may have pushed Christianity, or like programs, a bit hard for some of the miners. It was possible too, that management hesitated to accept miners on the men's own terms wishing to wash the unwashed! Whatever the reasons were, they caused discontent.]

Before I was married I did not do anything for relaxation but before I left the Northern Pacific I had won two tennis tournaments, city tournaments, not state. Mr. Herron very kindly had a tennis court built just outside my office in the Boarding House.

I cannot remember any Christmas the first year I was there alone, but after she [my wife] came the wives of the staff foremen did something about it. My wife had a piano and one day, hearing a small group of miners singing as they came from shift asked me who they were. I told her they were Cousin Jacks' [13] *who roomed together. She had me bring them up to our cabin and asked them if they knew any Christmas carols. They certainly did, and said they would sing* Hark the Herald Angels Sing *first. [As] they gave [sung] it, it was "Ard the Erald Hangels Sing." They had a very good choir and took great pride in it.* [14]

Yes, there was some high grading ore thefts [15] *but the one I knew more about, the party was caught and [recovered] most of the high grade ore from where his wife had hidden it. I think the higher grade ore were found at the upper levels of the mine.*

[Exploration for new ore veins and pockets continually went on in mines. The future of operations depended on what was or was not found. This proved an expensive and time-consuming effort.

The company that ignored exploration would not stay in business very long, once its first discoveries were mined out. Botkin knew this and wrote.] "The manager had us a drilling down some 2,500 feet to see if they could find good ore but this proved a failure as far as finding gold."

[Alex Botkin then repeated the story of the check and Thyra (whose picture is found in *Tomboy Bride* carrying the mail). He then continued with the dance story with a slight variation.]

> *When Mr. Herron decided to give the dance at the Tomboy Boarding house and the wives of the staff and foremen did such a wonderful job of decoration we did not include the shift bosses and their wives. The morning following the dance the wife of one of the shift bosses came to my office to see me. When I asked her what I could do for her she said she wanted to know why the shift bosses and their wives had not been invited. I tried to explain to her that we didn't want more hosts than possible guests. Whereupon she said, "where me and Henry come from we're used to hoeing [socializing or dancing] with the best" and stamped out.*

> *Of course life at the Tomboy, as interesting as it was, was not without some unpleasantries due in almost every case, to some misunderstanding, but I believe the Tomboy Mine and its management would rank high for fair play.*

> *You no doubt know all about the famous reply to the governor [James Peabody] when he sent a member of the legislature to Telluride to investigate the causes for the trouble the Tomboy was having with labor. His report was in effect "militia unnecessary, miners*

in peaceful possession of the property." This was before I went there.

For sometime I was the oldest man here in this home but a man has recently entered who is six months older than I am. I have received three gifts of sympathy from some sisters who consider that I am now only a has-been.

Wishing you a happy new year and if I should recall any story I have not sent you I will do so.

Sincerely,

A. W. Botkin

Apr. 28th, 1973

Dear Mr. Smith,

In reply to your letter of the 23rd let me answer your questions first. The store at the Tomboy was a very small affair in charge of a man we knew as Scotty. He carried only such clothing as a miner may need, tobacco in all forms, and such well organized remedies such as you might have in your home. The mail for the Tomboy came to the Smuggler Union [16] by tram and it was Scotty's duty each day to go to the Smuggler Union on horseback for the Tomboy mail.

There was a tennis court [17] in Telluride where I had played some before Mr. Herron had the one at the Tomboy built but the altitude never seemed to bother me. The miners had the bowling alley built during the Y.M.C.A. and later, but their main activity was the gambling at the store.

[Here Alex explains further the problems he encountered between two sets of bosses.]

When I worked for the Tomboy, the Supt. D. A. Herron [18] *explained to me that my immediate boss would be Mr. Tobin, who had charge of the Telluride office and that I was to follow his instructions and ask him for any information I wanted. Tobin was a very thorough man in every particular, but he was a gambler in Telluride and could hardly be approached when so engaged. However I never heard a word of any complaint from Supt. Herron. On one or two occasions I found myself in a position following one boss when not entirely in agreement with the other. Only on one occasion did I accompany the shipments of gold to Telluride.*

I cannot recall any company coming to the mine in the role of actors or lecturers or locally [produced plays]. I cannot remember that there was any restriction on the possession of whiskey by staff members, who might have occasion to entertain guests as my wife did on many occasions. However I might add that most whiskey would be found as a medicine.

I recall one instance my wife was guest to a woman who I think was from Wisconsin University and went to the Tomboy in her capacity as a professor there. Mr. Herron showed [her] all she wanted to know about the mine and mill and how we go our water supply, etc. Then he took her up to our log house to meet my wife in our home.

She told us Mr. Herron had been so generous and gave all she wanted to know, but she had never dreamed that she was to be so delightfully entertained as she was by my wife, who could tell her much about the lives of married miners and their families. She said we had made a really delightful home of our plain log cabin and this experience had been a delightful experience.

Many more visitors reached our log house in the same manner, many very interesting people among them. On one occasion the Supt. of the mine very near Telluride called me at my mine office. He was very inquisitive about the manner in which I kept my records and I told him that was all determined by the Telluride office. I suspected, and correctly, that he was more interested in what my records said than in what manner I kept them. So I simply told him that I was unable to furnish all the information he sought and that he would have to get it from the Telluride office.

Here at this home where I live much entertainment is furnished for the numerous elderly people. On occasions, an hour at a time, machine music of very old well known tunes are played, cards are available for play every day, bingo at times, etc. But this is not the Tomboy. I will be 98 years old later in July and have a great deal to be thankful for. I am the last member of my family and the oldest of the class of Sheffield Scientific School of 1899. We lost one about a month ago. He was 93. Our class secretary is now 94 so we did pretty well for a class of about 150 students.

Here comes an interruption so must close.

Yours very truly,

A. W. Botkin

In a short note to Harriet Backus, in May 1943, James Batcheller briefly described some of his remembrances. He focused on the mill cleanups during the prosperous years when both families were there. In an off-hand way, he listed a few interesting experiences.

There was some silver with the Tomboy gold. The gold bars weighed eighty-five to ninety pounds avoirdupois, were 4" wide 3 1/2-4 deep, by 9" and were worth $25,000,-$30,000. I left in August 1909, and before that if the ore was particularly good — amalgam was accumulated in the mine office safe until there was enough to make two to three bars — all that the mule pack saddle safely could hold in one filling. Then there was Bullion Day. Often there would be three cleanups a month. I do not ever recall less than two of two bars each.

Mildred Ekman did not think she had many memories to share, but it turned out that she did repeat several about her Tomboy and Telluride childhood.

Grand Junction, Colo.

June 18, '74

It has been a month since I received your letter so should at least answer.

It was nice of you to write to me. I wish I could help you but I really don't know what I could say. If someone was around and we would be talking about Tomboy, and each one would remember a little, I am sure a lot of things would come out.

Mrs. Backus sure got a lot into her book. I wrote her and told about a few things, she said she wished we could have gotten together. I was not very old at the time she was first married and lived there but I do remember a lot about her story.

I have tried to think of someone that would have been there, but our family moved up and down to Tomboy several times. My dad always wanted to get away from mining, but always came back. [19]

[Mildred's dad was pretty typical. A lot of men wanted to get away from the hard work, dangers, and health risks of mining, but could not quite do it. Not only did the pay prove better than many jobs, but mining got into, and still does, one's blood. There is a fascination, adventure, and excitement about working in a mine, plus a companionship with your partners, that seemed hard to overcome and return to the outer world.]

I just started school up there. Letta Teller was the teacher for the one room, first through eight. I remember one of the older boys. He was the largest in the room and his name was Eddie Small. Mrs. Teller played the organ and the kids always wanted her to play and sing "Juanita."

When we first were up there and all small, we liked all the pretty rocks. We lived by the shaft house in a little house and us kids would pick rocks from the dump and pile them behind the house to play with. (I still like pretty rocks.) My mother said one day the manager came to the house and said someone had reported that my dad was high-grading behind the house. She took him behind the house and he laughed and said let them play.

Mrs. Backus wrote about when my baby sister died. I remember that. I must have been between 5 and 6 years old. Mama got the baby dressed and ready for burial and tied her on a board and wrapped it up good. Her and my father rode down to Telluride on horseback, and she carried the baby on the saddle in front of her all the way to town.

I don't remember any special games we played. Kids then could find their fun. We would go up on the hill and throw rocks down old shafts and listen for them to hit the bottom or wherever they hit.

In the winter when we lived in one of the houses almost up to where the powder magazine [20] *was, the man (the Powder Monkey) came in the morning for the dynamite, in his one-horse sled. The kids would be on their way to school. He would stop, let us climb up on the boxes, help the small ones up, take us to the turn of the road, [where] we would pile off and head one way to school. He went the other way. Wonder what a mining company now-a-days would do if kids even got close to the dynamite.*

There was a lot of fun for all at the club [she was not clear if she was referring to some organization at the Tomboy or in Telluride]. *No one worried about baby sitters, as the kids got sleepy they were piled on top of coats until everyone was ready to leave.*

I told Mrs. Backus it is too bad so many old ones are gone when someone starts to write about what used to be.

Sincerely,

Mildred Matson Ekman

Martha Gibbs clearly remembered her Telluride childhood. With enthusiasm she wrote me about those days.

> Box 567
> Colfax, Cal 95713
>
> August 22, 1974
>
> To say that I was interested in your letter would be putting it mildly. If you can read around the typographical errors and erasures I will write what I can about life in Telluride as a little girl growing up around the turn of the century. This will be a joint venture with my younger sister, Eloise, who is just 80. I am a year older.
>
> I was quite ill last November and she came down and together we sold, gave away or brought with us the accumulation of 45 years of housekeeping. Then in February I had surgery for cataracts and together they make me very uncertain on the typewriter. Although I earned my livelihood doing office work (45 years).
>
> I loved Tomboy Bride and wrote to her (Mrs. Backus) that I recall many things that she mentioned like Kracaw's Grocery Store and the livery stable and other things.
>
> I will write a few memories on a separate sheet and if you decide you can use more I will send it a little at a time.
>
> With every good wish for your "research," I remain
>
> Yours very truly
>
> Martha Lee Gibbs

She included in the letter a separate page entitled "Things I Remember."

"Ladies" did not call each other by their given names no matter how long they knew each other or how well. It was "Mrs. Gibbs" and "Mrs. Kirby" with Mother's best friend and neighbor all the years we lived in Telluride. They kept in touch over the years and they were still "Mrs. Gibbs" and "Mrs. Kirby."

Our house stood on the same street as the High School only at the other end. I don't remember the street names but I think I can get them for you. My grand nephew and his wife have made two trips over there in the last 7 years. Our house has a porch along the front of the house and was originally built without a kitchen or bath. Four rooms downstairs and two up. Living room and dining-room-and-kitchen on one side and two bedrooms on the other. The kitchen [apparently at this point another kitchen was added completely separate from the combination used before] *and bath were added later eliminating the necessity for a "Chic Sales"* [21] *tho they did not call it that in those days. If you don't know, I'll tell you!*

We burned soft and hard coal. The latter was for a huge base burner in the living room. Dad would get up early and shake down the ashes and take out the "clinkers" and sit down to read. His idea of light reading was the Engineering News [22] *to which he had earlier contributed a story and drawings. If we girls who had the bedrooms upstairs didn't get up when he called, it made [for] a good "hurry up" and get up signal.*

Our lot sloped from the back to the front leaving about three feet of sharp slope where he [Dad] planted clover and we spent many happy hours making bouquets of the blossoms. There was a fence around the house, 3 rows of 1x4 with a topping of a board put on so we couldn't walk on the top. We walked on the board, so he took it off to prevent that and we walked on the 1" top edge. There was a big window in the dining room and hop vines over that, so it was leafy and cool in the summer.

There was a hill alongside the house (we were on the corner) and we used to come home and take a slide before we went back to school. Dad scorned the flat iron [sled] runners that were used in those days so he got round runners, which were much faster than the others. Most of the sleds around were about 8 inches high with the flat runners. Our sled was 4 inches high (and would carry 3). He [Dad] had a bobsled, which would carry 6 or 8 adults. It was of 2x12 (or 15") lumber beveled and finished very smoothly. He made it in two sections so we could use the front for separate trip, which we girls did very often. He never got around to painting it. Frequently they [the parents] and a few of their friends would spend the evening "sledding" on a steeper hill than that near us and then they would come back to our place to [cook] "shrimp wiggle" cooked up in the chafing dish.

We all attended the school at the other end of the street. I was subject to bronchitis and Mother would get me ready and send me out ahead of the others. But I would wait for them at the next corner and then we would all have to run to get there in time. At recess we had the grounds marked up with hopscotch both round and straight. (If you have never seen these let me know and I will draw some for you. I do not know how long they have lasted in this year 1974).

[1] Yale's approach to mining education was more like a series of lectures on mining, rather than offering a degree program. Therefore, graduates, like Botkin, took another major and did additional work at another institution.

[2] Beth and Jim Batcheller were good friends of Harriet and George and play a major role in *Tomboy Bride*.

[3] Amalgam balls came from the combining of mercury with the gold ore from the Tomboy, which had been crushed in the mill. Mercury, or quicksilver, has a natural affinity for gold and will combine with it. The resulting ball would be heated driving the mercury off, where it would be recovered, leaving behind the gold and what little silver might be combined with it.

[4] The narrow trail, with mountains on one side and a drop off into the valley on the other and no intersecting trails, made it relatively safe to ship gold from Savage Basin down to Telluride. The jeep road to the mine follows the same trail and it is easy to see why robberies did not occur.

[5] The *San Miguel Examiner,* March 22, 1909, went into more detail about freighting. Hauling and packing Tomboy concentrates all the time, "keeps Ed Lavender's freight outfits busy." Lavender was working anywhere from fifty to one hundred animals every day, "some of them make two trips daily." To concentrate ore, meant separating ore from its "containing rock or earth." The ratio varied, but for example, a mill might crush eight tons of rock and, after separating out the waste material, leave two tons of enriched ore. This cut the number of tons that needed to be shipped.

[6] Baseball was extremely popular in the mining communities, a team played for town honor and to win the bets local fans placed on the game's winning outcome. The editor of the *San Miguel Examiner* (May 18, 1907) bemoaned "the prospects for the national game in Telluride this summer are rather discouraging." Still, throughout the 1906-10 years, Telluride fielded a nine that took on teams from all the surrounding communities.

[7] James Peabody was first elected governor of Colorado in 1902, and then lost a reelection bid in a controversial contest in 1904. After an investigation, it was ruled he had won, both parties being guilty of election fraud, and the governor resigned. As part of the compromise to end the turmoil and controversy, Peabody agreed to resign within twenty-four hours. He did and was replaced by the lieutenant governor, Jesse McDonald, thus, Colorado had three governors in one day. Pro-business Peabody had served during the vicious 1903-04 strikes and backed the owners throughout with all the might of the state government.

[8] Telluride's population ranged from a high in 1900 of 2,446 downward to 1,756 in 1910. During these years, the first major mining decade in its history, it was the largest community in the San Juan mining region.

[9] Highly respected John Herron survived the labor struggles and brought the Tomboy back into full production after the 1903-04 strike. Herron had

formerly been general manager of the Drumlummon Mine in Montana. He had been appointed general superintendent of the Tomboy in July 1898. The London directors thought so much of him that they voted Herron a 2,000 pounds bonus. *Engineering and Mining Journal,* January 10, 1902.

[10] Tobin, as identified later, was also a gambler, an unusual occupation for someone employed in a mining office. A check of the *Colorado Business Directories,* 1906-10, failed to produce a Tobin at Telluride. There was question about abolishing the Telluride office and combining it with the office at the mine. One reason the Company kept the former was "relations with the community."

[11] Bob Meldrum, a feared killer and company guard, had been deputized during the strike. He made his Telluride debut in a striking manner. Shouldering up to the bar at the Union Saloon, he announced. "I'm Bob Meldrum. You can always find me when you want me. Now if any son of a bitch has anything to say, spit it out; otherwise, I'm going to take a drink — and alone." How and why he died is a mystery. See John R. Burroughs, "Bob Meldrum, Killer for Hire," *Denver Post,* September 23, 1962.

[12] The *San Miguel Examiner,* November 24, 1906, announced that YMCA buildings at the Tomboy and Smuggler would be "dedicated this week." The June 1, 1907, issue reported the YMCA association "is showing much life and hustle," with the "educational classes well patronized." In May 1908, the paper noted that the Tomboy had 127 members with a bowling alley, pool tables, athletic apparatus and the like available. The Smuggler and the Tomboy held bowling tournaments against each other.

[13] Cornish miners, nicknamed "Cousin Jacks," were considered some of the best miners available. Coming from the long heritage of mining in Cornwall, England, they scattered throughout the world as the mines in their home country closed. If a mine had a Cornish supervisor or shift boss usually a majority of the crew were Cornish. Their wives were often known as "Cousin Jennies."

[14] Cornish choirs were famous throughout the West. Central City, Colorado and Grass Valley, California, for example, had noted ones. The Cornish were also noted for their pasties, meat (pies), superstitions, and strong Methodist leanings.

[15] Stealing of ore, "high grading," was developed into an art by miners in the West. False bottom lunch buckets, and hallow boot heels were just two of the ways the ore disappeared after a shift in the mine. High-grade ore was the richest found in a mine and the ore was sold as specimens or bullion.

[16] The famous Smuggler Union Mine was in Marshall Basin, slightly north and west of the Tomboy and above it in altitude. While, unfortunately, only partial production figures remain for this property, it rivaled the Tomboy in fame and fortune. In May 1901, a strike broke out here that left a great deal of bitterness among both the miners and owners and led to the 1903-04 struggle for control of the district.

[17] Alex Botkin was a good tennis player. He and a partner won the Telluride doubles tennis tournament on July 4, 1908. That same day, while the Tomboy

baseball team did not play, the Smuggler nine won two games including beating the Liberty Bell team.

[18] David Herron also was manager of the Tomboy. He closed the mine in 1927.

[19] Mining got in their "blood," and no matter how they might wish to try another occupation, they went back. The major problem for them was the physical stress and danger, which often aged them prematurely despite all the monetary advantages. "Old" miners in their late thirties and forties were only rarely found still working in the nineteenth century. Accidents and miner's consumption also took a toll.

[20] For obvious reasons, the powder house, or magazine, that stored explosives was located away from the main buildings. The person employed to distribute dynamite and fuse to the miners was the powder monkey. Interestingly, this is a nautical term used in the mining industry.

[21] Apparently, she is referring to an outhouse.

[22] It would seem that she is referring to the *Engineering and Mining Journal,* the leading industry journal of the day.

A Time for Yesterday's Shadows

Both Harriet and her grandson, Rob, generously shared photographs of their family and the Tomboy days with me. They provide the heart of this glimpse into the past. The photographs actually cover nearly a century, as the last ones were taken on a trip to the Tomboy site on September 13, 2002.

Little remains today to explain what occurred in Savage Basin in those long ago days, only the fleeting shadows of what once was and will never be again. The buildings have nearly collapsed, victims of an unfair struggle with unrelenting nature. The snow Harriet remembered, the wind, and the passage of years have left little. Then came the tourists picking up what once had been discarded and now proclaimed to be a first class souvenir. Some of the buildings were knocked down to avoid becoming an "attractive nuisance." Man did his share in another way as well with an environmental cleanup so that the water cascading down into the valley would not pollute. Only sites and hollow shells remain along with the dumps of waste rock.

Looking about the ruin that once had so much life, one is reminded of Percy Shelley's sonnet "Ozymandias." It described a traveler who happened upon a broken statue in the desert which had these words inscribed upon it.

"My name is Ozymandias, King of Kings;
Look on my works, ye Mighty, and despair!"
Nothing beside remains. Round the decay
Of that colossal wreck, boundless and bare
The lone and level sands stretch far away.

#963   09-25-2015 3:34PM
Item(s) checked out to p1318155.

TITLE: A visit with the Tomboy Bride : H
BARCODE: 109000736097
DUE DATE: 10-16-15

TITLE: Nothing daunted [sound recording]
BARCODE: 1240051091662
DUE DATE: 10-02-15

TITLE: Half broke horses [sound recordin
BARCODE: 109000908461
DUE DATE: 10-02-15

Renew online at http://gcld.org
Hot Sulphur Springs Library 725-3942

Not sand, but mountains guard the once mighty Tomboy Mine.

The only way to recapture all this is through the written word and scrutinizing the photographs, which remain. The author of "Ecclesiastes" wrote: "For everything there is a season and a time for every matter under heaven: a time to weep and a time to laugh; a time to seek, and a time to lose; and a time to throw away stones, and a time to gather stones together." All this has transpired.

A smattering of the mined "stones" became gold while other "stones" collected on the mine dumps and mill tailings. A few eventually were taken home as souvenirs by inquisitive tourists. The seeking has ceased, and the losing happened generations ago. The laughter and crying have faded, but grieve not, a few shadows remain. By studying the photographs that follow, at least a bit of the saga emerges into view.

Harriet Backus, c1907. Courtesy: Smith/Walton

George Backus, c1916. Courtesy: Rob Walton

Harriet Backus. Courtesy: Rob Walton

Harriet Backus. Courtesy: Rob Walton

The Tomboy Mine in the Backus era. Courtesy: Smith/Backus

Harriet well remembered winter at the Tomboy. Courtesy: Rob Walton

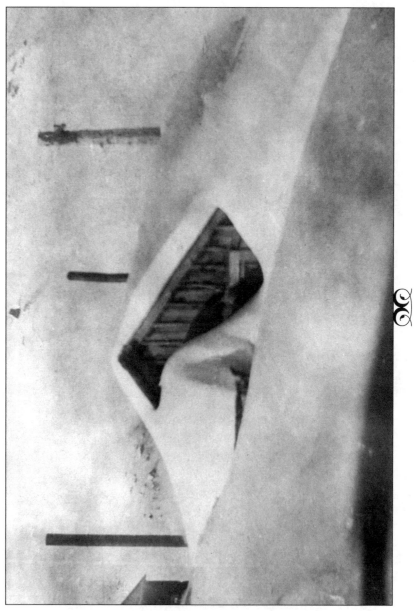

A cabin next to Beth and Jim Batcheller's house. Harriet remarked that "the man had to tunnel out to get to work many times." Courtesy: Smith/Backus

Savage Basin and the Tomboy Mine taken from the vicinity of the Big Elephant Slide. Courtesy: Duane A. Smith

Announcement of daughter Harriet Backus's birth.
Courtesy: Rob Walton

Mother Harriet and daughter Harriet at the Tomboy.
Courtesy: Rob Walton

"Castle Sky High" in the circle where George and Harriet lived 1906-10. Courtesy: Smith/Backus

"Tunnel of Love" on the Tomboy road. Courtesy: Rob Walton

Gold ore coming down from the Tomboy to Telluride. Courtesy: Duane A. Smith

Pack trains like this hauled supplies to the mine and the families living in Savage Basin. Courtesy: Smith/Backus

Harriet and George attended some of the Tomboy parties. This one was set for a Thanksgiving banquet. Courtesy: Barbara Hosner

Telluride nestled in a mountain surrounded valley several thousand feet below the Tomboy and Savage Basin. The mills sit in the foreground, Telluride in the background around the turn-of-the-century. Courtesy: U. S. Forest Service

Telluride in the early 1900s when Harriet and George occasionally
came to town. Courtesy: P. David Smith

Telluride's Community Hospital where Harriet was born. The Western Federation of Miners built a second hospital before they were driven out of the district. Courtesy: Duane A. Smith

Harriet and George Backus, c1939. Courtesy: Rob Walton

Just a few of the men who worked at the Tomboy posed before the boarding-house for the photographer. Courtesy: Chris Buys

An immense cascade of sludge filled Telluride's Colorado Avenue during the 1914 flood. Courtesy: P. David Smith

The New Sheridan's lavish bar was filled with slimy mud and other debris from the 1914 flood. Courtesy: P. David Smith

The Tomboy in the 1970s, when more structures showed that man lived there once. Even then it was a favorite stopping place for people traveling over the popular Tomboy/Imogene Pass road from Telluride to Ouray. [Three photographs] Courtesy: Duane A. Smith

Looking across from the Pennsylvania Tunnel into Savage Basin and the Tomboy site. Nature works diligently in the process of reclaiming its own. Courtesy: John Ninnemann

Weather, vandalism, and an environmental cleanup have taken their
toll. Twenty years ago, the assay office was standing.
Courtesy: Glen Crandall

A few cabins still withstand against encroaching time in September 2002. Courtesy: John Ninnemann

A tunnel to the Tomboy is still open, a dangerous invitation to
unaware tourists. Courtesy: John Ninnemann

An ore car, twisted tracks and other debris outside the assaying
furnace. Courtesy: John Ninnemann

The foundation of the mill still stands like a row of rock grave markers. Courtesy: John Ninnemann

CHAPTER 4
Trials and Tribulations

These letters[1], including one from George to Harriet, discuss other events in which she was not involved. They provide insights into life in the San Juans including Telluride's 1914 flood, a trip across the mountains, and the condition of mining in some of the declining districts.

The July 14, 1914, flood ranks as one of the great natural disasters to hit Telluride. A cloudburst of epic proportions dumped continuous rain high above Cornet Creek. A swirling, leaping, mass of water raced downward sweeping everything before it, carrying rocks, trees, and the ruined remains of man made structures. Crashing down the creek, the brownish-gray ooze surged into Telluride with a terrifying roar. Terrified animals and people ran for their lives as buildings and homes were knocked off their foundations.[2] Beth Batcheller (to whom the letter was addressed) and you can both read first hand what happened. This letter from Mrs. W. B. Nicodemus to Beth Batcheller recounts the devastating 1914 flood.

Mrs. W. B. Nicodemus to Mrs. J. H. Batcheller
Aug 6, 1914
Dear Mrs. Batcheller:

Your check received yesterday. I'm sure my dear it can be put to good use. I turned it over to the Relief Committee — composed of E. B. Adams, J. M. Woyt, W. A. Nicodemus.

I'll try to tell you how we saw it [the flood]. Will had just started by the office — about 1 P.M. He was at the front door and called to me, "What is this noise?" I was in the kitchen with Sandy and heard nothing and wouldn't have, I suppose, until it was upon us. When I got to the front door I heard a crack and saw it go over the little house across the street from Lehvan's, Oscar Wunderlick came across and I could hear the water roaring and I said, "We must run" for it looked as if it was coming right at us. We ran out the alley. Will had stopped to get a coat for Sandy for it was raining and S and I started down towards Haulons and Will called me to go up the alley or S and I would have been caught in the torrent. So we went up to the side [of the hill?] along the hospital. I looked back when we got to the end of our alley and I saw that awful torrent coming back of Litchfield's, Haulon's, destroying their homes. I could only think, "Oh God save our home." It divided and one side of the torrent went in front of Litchfield's and Haulon's and through the back of Waggoners' yard, simply ploughing it up and on through the next yard wrecking that little house that stood next to the Nurse's Union hospital and on oh, I can't tell you just where but part went as far as the Catholic Church and went down that way filling houses with mud. The street in front of Waggoner's filled almost and Main Street, all in front of McMahons' home that you lived in and on the side clear to the fence in the back is filled. The house that the Johnsons lived in, just across the street, is entirely gone and the little house just between it and the Science Church is washed up against the church and almost torn to pieces. The house you will remember that the ill-fated St. James lived in is surrounded with mud 3 or 4 feet but the house is standing. Litchfields' and Haulons' — the back part of their houses torn away and the rest of the house torn apart by

boulders and just filled with mud. Its parlor and liv-
ing room have no mud. What is left of the house is
twisted to one side. The little house across the street
on the corner from Litchfields' is turned and tipped
forward. Mrs. Bengston's house is entirely washed
away. The woman who was living in it was badly
hurt but is recovering. Mrs. Bengston and her family
have lived out in a part of the Wells' house all win-
ter. Lehman's little house that stood next to
Bengston's was washed way over and all caved in.
Lehman's big house is upset but the furniture was all
right. The woman who lived in Lehman's little house
was killed. She and her husband were running and a
boulder knocked her down and I supposed killed her.
She was found against that little white house just
across the street from us.

Your yard and the Redick house and Gevais are a
mass of boulders — not a square inch in either that
isn't covered.

When one stream went down Oak Street — in front
of Lehman's—it took that house on the corner next
to Lehmans went on down and filled all the houses
on the east side of that street, Dr. Cross, McKown's
and the McDonalds — only their yard and not their
house. Then it made as neat a turn as a buggy would
make at the Methodist Church, went back of it
[church] filling Jarvis yard and wrecking the first
floor of the Annex — up on this side towards us —
it filled up that alley from the Sheridan to Byers'
Studio and ran through the Sheridan dining room
into the office and on to Main St. The same way
through the cafe and bar, the Phoenix Market, the
old Princess Picture Show, Gauek Saloon and the

room formerly occupied by the Samson Drug Store and filling Main St. There its strength seemed to have been spent. There was a pile in Main St. averaging four feet from the Sheridan to the First National Corner. My dear, the cafe and barroom were the most awful sights. They were filled with that awful mud to within a foot of the ceiling. Poor Mr. Segerberg, his loss is so heavy. Mrs. Blakeley, who was killed, was the wife of [two words unreadable].[3] The space between Litchfields' and our house is a mass of rocks and timber. There was a pile of mud along our sunroom to the bedroom to the windows but we have cleared that away.

In the back yard only a little round on that side by Litchfields where the rose bushes are — the rose bushes are covered. [She included a map here, but it was too faint to reproduce.]

Will received Mr. B's kind letter and will reply as soon as he has time. He is so busy now with this committee work. Mrs. Wells and the girls are over at Electra [4] now and the boys too and [illegible word] Mr. Wells. He was over with them once before.

She [Grace Wells] seems happy. The day of the flood she was down and she said she must hurry back and Mr. W made her promise she would be back with the girls before dark. Also spoke of how nice it was they [were] all together. I've seen her only twice. They've had a house full of company. My nephew, Dan Cunninghamm, was here a month. The dear boy. 18 years old. He and Elizabeth Herron had grand times together. I almost perished when he left. I'll write you a different kind of letter next time but I *thought maybe I would explain the situation a little. I'll send you some pictures when the Byers[5] gets them made. I know I've made all sorts of mistakes in this letter. Some I am in time to correct but others will have to go.*

Oh I forgot to show you how it left Huzzie — it went right back of them—left them high and dry. [She included her a little hand drawn map.]

Ever thine,

A second letter to Beth arrived from Mary Waggoner, whose house was untouched, giving another vivid description of the flood.

August 5, 1914

Dearest Mrs. Batcheller:

Your letter came last night.

We are in the heart of the stricken district and such desolation you cannot imagine. Thou we are safe ourselves and by good luck our house wasn't touched, but the back yard up to the porch is a ruin.

When I was sending out "Journals" containing the account of the flood I thot[6] of you but did not send one because I thot Mrs. Nick would. I was at her house when she received your telegram and naturally supposed that of course she would send you a paper. I asked her last night and she said "No, she had not" so Mr. Waggoner said he would get one today to send to you. It contains a very true account. Contrary to all expectations, the flood did not touch any thing west of Oak Street so Mrs. Houser, Moys, Herrons were all safe. Mr. Herron was at the mine but came tearing down. Someone at the Liberty Bell Mine saw the cloud burst at the top of Saw Tooth Range and telephoned to town and all the people in the west end were warned by telephone and the ringing of the fire bell. No one supposed it would go where it did so we who were in its path never received one word of warning. It seems that the course it took was the old riverbed. You know the west wall of the Cornet Canon is a solid mass of rock while this side is soft earth, so naturally when this roaring mass of boulders and trees came down it took the path of least resistance tearing out the dam and part of the hillside. It first took out Oscar Wunderlick's then came diagonally across Oak Street taking Celnuaie's and the two cottages next to it toward the hill and a little corner of Mary Morgan's house. It then made a straight shot down to Litchfield's corner, demolishing their house, also Mr. Haulon's and carried Marie Johnson's house completely away Marie escaping after the house began to move. It just struck Mrs. Nick's yard but did no damage to the house. At Litchfield's corner it branched, coming straight from their corner to the corner of our fence on the alley tearing that out, also our chicken coop and filled out back yard up to the porch, but none came into the house or cellar and neither is the barn damaged except for the door on the alley being torn off. Fortunately, no mud got into the coal bins. It continued its way thru Baker's yard next door, tearing out the shed on the back of the house and filled the cellar with mud but did no further damage except to the yard. The house next to the Union Hospital is a wreck and the hospital well filled with mud. It crossed the street at Baker's going into the

Iowa house and into Updegraff's on the opposite corner continuing with small force at Main Street.

It also came down the street by our house, *filling the street to the top of our hitching post and almost to the top of our picket fence but it scarcely rose through the pickets so our house wasn't touched on that side. It just touched the McMahon house you lived in but did no damage. The Redich house is surrounded but not damaged nor none inside. The Gervais house is also surrounded and cellar filled. There are boulders in our yard that will weigh a ton.*

The flood also went down Oak St. but did no damage except on the east side. All the people who lived from Ledman's corner to the Methodist Church were driven out and their homes filled with mud. The Misses McDonald escaped thou[gh] they were surrounded front and back. The Charlie Painter and Fitzgerald houses escaped too.

Delos and Francis Dalle had been riding on Delos' filly and had gone to put her horse in the stable. Before they got back it began to rain and Delos planned that he would wait at Mr. Dalle's store until the rain was over.

It soon began to pour and the thunder and lightning were so bad I shut off the current in my electric range. I then went into the pantry and heard a terrific roaring. I thot that must be a larger mud slide than usual (we have had so many little mud slides on the hills this summer) so I got an umbrella and went out in the back yard. Mrs. Baker came out and said, "What is it, Mrs. Waggoner?"

Very unconcernedly I informed her I thot it must be a cloud burst up Cornet Creek but it never occurred to me that it would come our way or even be much of anything no matter what its course. We stood looking for a few minutes and then I said I would go in to get my opera glasses to see if I could see anything. As I started into the back door Mrs. Litchfield, Edwin and the Grandmother came tearing out of their house and Mrs. Litchfield shrieked, "Run for your life, Mrs. Waggoner." I saw their house move but could not see what moved it and wondered if the noise I heard could have been an explosion and fire in Litchfield's house. I ran into the house, calling Sultan and dashed upstairs for my rings and out the front door grabbing an umbrella as I ran. By this time the Litchfields' were at our corner and I took the Grandmother under my umbrella and found we were in the path of the cloud-burst. We stood there for some minutes it seemed and the water had begun to run down Galena past our house but not down in front of the house. The man in Redick's house, Mr. Decker, came and told me to take Mrs. Litchfield into my house that all danger was passed and our house was safe. Mr. Lawson heard him and said, "Don't you dare go into your house, go down town."

I ran down the street to the bank and met Mr. Waggoner running home. We both started for Delos, Mr. W. on one street and I on the other and when I arrived at Mr. Delos' store it was locked. I went back to the bank and found that locked. I know I'd never find the boys if I ran around so I waited on the corner of Van Otto's old store until the flood had reached the Iowa house. Fortunately, by this time its greatest force was spent and it came slowly, but I crossed over to Lapin's corner and soon Delos came. His father had found him up on the hill at Mrs. Dalle's where they had gone when the excitement began. I said we would wait until the flood came to the middle of the block and then we would make for the hill across the river. Just then Mr. Waggoner came and we rushed to the stable where Delos and Mr. Waggoner saddled the horses while John Carrol, whom we had picked up and I stood guard. I then took the horses and the two boys to San Miguel City where I left them but I came right back to town with Mr. Brown. When we got to Mrs. Work's corner on Oak Street we met Mr. Lehman and Mr. Brown said, "How is the Waggoner house?" Mr. Lehman replied, "I saw Delos a little bit ago and he said he saw his house go." We rode on down to Pacific Ave. The only street running east and west that was possible and the mud and water there came to our horses knees at times, and there we met Mr. Waggoner who said our house was to all appearances all right and he was going to get rubber boots to try to get up to it. The boy and I stayed at San Miguel that night.

The next day I remarked to him the strange thing people in their excitement said and told him about Mr. Lehman's remark. Delos said no, he had told half a dozen people our house was gone, for when he left to join us, this great wall of mud almost as high as the fence was sweeping around the corner of our fence over the sidewalk and thru Baker's yard so he couldn't see how our house could escape. But Heaven be Praised! We did escape and so did the rest of our property. The nurse's cottage wasn't touched, neither was the hospital. The barn in which we keep our horses was entirely surrounded but the barn itself is all right and the floor dry.

I hope you won't be worried to death reading this and if there are misspelled words or words omitted please overlook it and supply from your own imagination. I am thankful you were not here with your two boys and glad Mrs. Lervais had left here too. Much love to you all and kiss the two boys for me and tell Edgar "Waggin" would like to see him and Robin.

I have been miserable for months but am taking a tonic, which has helped me. The only evil effect of the flood has been an attack of sciatica the last three days.

Yours,
Mary L. Waggoner

This December 20, 1912, letter from F. E. Frothingham to Beth [unidentified, but possibly Beth Batcheller][7] was written from the Strater Hotel, Durango's outstanding hotel with "all modern conveniences." The segment included graphically illustrated wintertime dangers of those years, or any year for that matter, in the San Juans for those who had to travel through the mountains. The author despite his dangerous journey, still had admiration for the natural beauty. His description of the snowslide he nearly got caught in is as close to one as any of us would probably care to find ourselves.

I asked the men to telephone you from Red Mountain that the trip across the pass was successfully accomplished, but the telephones were out of order and it was necessary to go on. My legs were fine but my breath was bad, so that we moved slowly in the higher levels. Two hours and forty minutes from the Tom Boy[8] to Lake Ptarmigan a half hour stop there, and then 1 hour and three quarters to Red Mountain. If only the numerous photographs I took between the Tom Boy and the lake come out I shall be delighted.

The best thing in the trip was the dinner your good husband gave us, and the second best was escaping the slides as we went down. These were splendid, if fearful. The sun was below the mountain as we were winding our way down steep slopes. Roy, who went first, advised against a comparatively easy looking depression under the towering shoulder of the mountain, so we kept above it and away from the great snowfield. Suddenly the snow cracked under us and we stopped instinctively. Nothing further happened under us, but as we looked up a shimmering white line darted across the pale snow slope opposite and in another moment a great slide had begun. The seething sound increased with the speed; down it came sweeping in a splendid curve into the hollow we had avoided swept across it, up the other side, and then like the spray of the sea appeared over a shoulder just below us and swept up, within 100 feet of where we stood.

Our way ahead took us down a very sharp incline toward exposed rocky shoulders, where the drop was precipitous and wicked. We had to skirt this to the right and cross the face of the further end of the slope from which the slide we had just watched had dislodged. We were all sobered, and the greater danger of the slide removed from me the fear I would otherwise have had of losing my footing on the steep slope we were crossing and rolling over the rocky rim. We spread apart, Roy leading the other man next and I last, so that the same thing could not happen to all three of us. Slowly Roy went on down and across over the dangerous slope. When he was well along he shouted for us to come fast. Two other men were coming up from below to meet us and were perhaps a quarter of a mile away. They were taking the place of a man who had started ahead of them and had been caught in the side of a small slide we could see ahead. He had managed to get out and to camp with a dislocated shoulder.

Scarcely had Roy called out for us to come on—we were strung along on the same slope—when a crack was heard above and we stood silent looking. Down it came. We could not evade anything anyway in the world. It started just ahead, the crack coming toward us. It was a wonderful wave came sweeping down. When it was nearly to us Roy shouted, "Boys, its got me" and I watched with a calmness that even then astonished me, to see him disappear and the wave go over the edge. With a diminishing seething it stopped, the lip of the wave burying the rocky rim, and Roy still standing with the farthest thrown pieces at his knees. The men coming up were almost as near. As we walked over the slide, broke and hard under our shoes, we estimated it 600 feet broad. We were safe crossing it and then quietly and steadily we went on across another quarter of a mile where the same danger was as imminent over the other slide, and down and around and into the timber. The worst timber will always have a new meaning to me. The rest of the way was moonlit beauty indescribable.

I did not mean to tire you with so much of this. What happened I suppose was only what happens to the strong men who dare these places the winter through. To me however it was a keen experience I would not have missed as it came out for a good deal. I remember wondering as I watched Roy, if it would "get me" too.

Now don't tell this story—it might reach Mother and I have probably made a mountain of it too. Roy would laugh at the tenderfoot.

The last segment is taken from a letter written by George to Harriet, dated September 23, 1909, describing part of his journey to Durango. He'd left Telluride at 6:30 am, "made it to Trout Lake by 2 pm and Lizard Head [pass] at 4pm." While not the adventure just described, George also had his problems traveling. The reader gains an appreciation of why the railroad saved the day, which brings up the question of why his party did not utilize the Rio Grande Southern.

From Lizard to Rico the road is more than rough. The load was quite heavy, a ton and 1/2 and we had four horses. Twice the wagon went into the mud up to the front axle and we had to unload the whole work to get out. Once we had to carry 6 sacks up a short steep pitch so the team could pull it over. One of us had to walk ahead to look at the road, as it was soon too dark to see. Ran into a boulder and broke the brake beam which took an hour to fix. Finally reached Rico at 2 AM this morning. Nothing to eat since we left Trout Lake a 2 PM in the afternoon.

We could not find anyone awake, finally found a bartender; he showed us a stable and woke up the landlady of a rooming house. He got the lady to cook us a little lunch. We put up the team, ate lunch and finally got to bed at 3:30AM. It was the worst bed I ever saw except at Uncle Sam Mine in Shasta Co. Cal. I woke up at 6 AM, could not stand the looks of the room or the comfort of the bed any longer so got up. Left there at 9:30 this morning.

Rico did not impress George, as one might imagine: "Rico is a deserted, broken down mining camp." What else he might have said is unknown because the rest of the letter was missing. Rico had seen better days by this time; in fact, it had slid twenty years past its prime and had never been one of the major San Juan communities, or districts, in the first place.[9]

---

[1] Loaned to me by Harriet Backus.

[2] For a graphic photographic history of this flood, see Chris Buys' *Historic Telluride*, 195-201

[3] Vera Blakeley went back to her home to rescue her dog, was trapped and smothered.

[4] There is an Electra Lake north of Durango above the Denver & Rio Grande tracks.

[5] Telluride photographer, J. Byers, took some famous photos of the flood.

[6] Not an uncommon abbreviation for the time — thought. Newspapers of the era used it frequently.

[7] Beth shared her letters with Harriet apparently to keep her up-to-date on San Juan matters.

[8] As mentioned early, the Tomboy was originally spelled Tom Boy. Apparently we have an individual here who continued to spell it that way.

[9] Rico's peak population had been 1,134 in 1890, by the time George arrived it had collapsed to 350 or so. Dolores County mining reflected its only important district Rico. Its top production had been in 1893 with $2.6 million, mostly silver. By the time George passed through, production had fallen to $110,000. Rico is a classic case of a district killed by the declining price of silver and the government going on the gold standard instead of the bimetal, silver and gold, standard. These factors produced the famous "Free Silver" issue of the 1870s-1890s era.

CHAPTER 5

Harriet's Trials of Writing a Book

Harriet Backus initially started her writing in the 1930s, then for various reasons, put it aside. She, meanwhile, asked the Batchellers for any remembrances they might have had. What they may, or may not, have contributed is unknown. She also obviously discussed her project with Alex Botkin who put her in touch with H. S. Canby, whom he thought might be able to help her get it published. He did not provide any direct help except encouragement. Harriet, however never gave up her dream even though she seemed to have doubts at times if she would ever succeed.

Harriet was excited about the prospect and in a July 1, 1974, letter explained her motivation to write her story.

I am sure you have known Mr. Henry Canby, a noted writer and one of the founders of the Saturday Review of Literature. *He was a close friend and Yale roommate of Alex Botkin.*

Back in the thirties I had written about our years at the Tomboy where we met Alex and his wife Kate. My idea was to write about further years so our children could have it but knowing how much these experiences meant to both the Batchellers and Botkins, I sent copies to them asking many questions. Alex was thrilled and right away sent a copy to Mr. Canby. The thought of doing that was far above my head but I received the letter from Mr. Canby which you have now and I, of course, was "puffed" right up to think such a noted literary man would even bother to read it.

Harriet Backus was not one to give up, however, as has been shown abundantly throughout her life. She told me about the trials she had publishing the book that finally led her to pay for the first edition. The success of *Tomboy Bride* abundantly rewarded her faith. There is no question she received much more pleasure from finding old friends and making new ones than from royalties. Repeatedly she mentioned to me how much fun she had corresponding with one and all. Before that happened, she had to find a publisher and the following two letters provide insights into her and publishing sixty years ago.

THE ALTAMONT
May 23, 1943

Hazleton, PA
Mr. H. S. Canby,
25 West 45th St.,
New York City, New York.

Dear Mr. Canby:

I have heard Alex Botkin speak of you so often that it seems easy to address you. He has asked me to send my manuscript direct to you. I hesitate to do so without your permission but Alex writes that he has explained to you that our moves are rapid and unexpected. [1]

I will explain briefly why I have written "our story." The first twelve years of our married life were spent in mining camps and made such a happy impression on my mind that the picture has never faded. There were three and a half years at the Tomboy, part of the time with Alex and Kate; then two years on the beautiful coast of British Columbia where there was nothing but a mill; next, one year in a remote part of Idaho to which we had to travel two days in an open stage coach; and finally five years in Leadville, Colorado, one of the most dramatic cities in the country.

My chapters on the last three locations are not as long as that on the Tomboy though to me they hold as much interest, as each had its individual charm.

I have always wanted to write of those twelve years for our children. Only the last few years have I found time. Four years ago Mr. Backus and I went to Australia and I wrote our family a complete account of that trip. After our return I started on our mining years. I so thoroughly enjoyed putting our experiences down on paper that I began to wonder if others might enjoy the reading of them.

If you see any merit in my account I would be happy to pay you for any advice you can give me. May I ask if you, yourself, revise such articles or, if not, and you feel that my manuscript is worth correcting, will you recommend someone to me?

I will deeply appreciate any advice or suggestions you will offer.

I was unable to get an experienced typist and I know there are many typographical errors and mistakes in punctuation which I have not taken time to correct.

If you find any interest in my narrative I would appreciate the privilege of meeting you. I can go to New York at your convenience for a brief discussion if you consider it worthwhile.

I am sending the manuscript to you by mail. When you return it will you please send it by express collect?

Harriet F. Backus

Saturday Review of Literature
25 West 45th Street, New York City

June 14, 1943

Mrs. George S. Backus
Altamont Hotel
Hazelton, Pennsylvania

My dear Mrs. Backus:

I have read with a great deal of pleasure your account of life at the mine. It is highly spirited, picturesque, and a real chapter in American experience. And of course I enjoyed meeting my dear friends the Botkins at the beginning of their career.

As for publishing it, I am a little doubtful. It is hard to publish a book in this wartime, unless there is a pretty certain demand for it. And the only judges of that demand are the publishers. I feel sure that this book would be of the greatest local interest in the Rocky Mountain region, if it could be published out there. Whether a general publisher would feel it were something he could handle would depend a great deal on the remainder of the book. I don't see that it needs any editing, except a certain amount of cutting, which would be easy to do. Frankly, the only thing I can advise is to pick out eight or ten good publishers who have handled books of this kind — and most publishers do — and try the manuscript on them. It is a slow process, but there is no short cut, because this is not the kind of book an agent could be helpful in placing.

I register at least my pleasure in reading this section.

Yours very truly,

Henry S. Canby

Fortunately, Harriet never lost faith and a quarter-of-a-century later *Tomboy Bride* appeared. Even then, she had to pay for the first edition. Nevertheless, her faith was abundantly rewarded with an excellent, most readable book that is still in print, eventual royalties, and an enjoyable decade catching up with some old friends and meeting and answering letters from new friends.

---

[1] It is unclear exactly what Harriet means with this statement. In the Tomboy era they moved frequently, but had been living in Oakland for years now. It is possible that George's work during World War II may have been such that they temporarily moved. Mrs. Backus never mentioned anything like that to me, although I did not ask her specifically about these years.

CHAPTER 6

The Legacy of the Tomboy Bride

For over a quarter-of-a-century, I have used *Tomboy Bride* as one of my assigned books in Colorado History. One of the questions I have used occasionally on tests follows. The students were to select A or B.

> A. What qualities made Harriet Backus an excellent mining camp wife? Be specific and support your conclusions with examples.

> B. What qualities made George Backus an excellent mining camp husband? Be specific and support your conclusions with examples.

Harriet and George have reached out and touched a generation far removed from their time and experiences. In all the years, I have required *Tomboy Bride* for my Colorado History class less than five students have evaluated it poorly. To give you the reader an idea of the Backuses' impact, a sampling of answers from the above questions are included. These are college students ranging from their early twenties into "non-trad," as the older students are described. They are all juniors or seniors, both women and men. I chose not to identify the students and cut their name off the text before I had it copied. Only the spelling has been corrected, after all under a timed test, spelling may find itself on the back burner!

— 1 —

Harriet Backus was an amazing woman because she stuck by her husband's side through everything. Harriet first left her home in Cal. to marry George in CO. She knew no one and had no idea what she was getting into. From there she lived at the Tomboy Mine through horrible winters, cooking, entertaining, and adjusting her life to be a miner's wife. She has no idea how to cook but she did; she had no idea how to survive in snow but she did. She loved all her new friends and neighbors. She went into the mine to see what her husband did — even though she was terrified. Harriet also lost one child of only two days but still moved on. Harriet would be accepting to anyone George brought home and never complained about cooking more food.

Harriet then moved on to Idaho to a very small town and she adjusted to that too. After a year they went to Butte, Montana and then finally to Leadville. She then took on substituting on the side and was always helping with house and the children. She loved her husband dearly through all the years and never complained (in the book). She was amazing for going on these crazy trips up trails of snow, helping others and most of all never leaving her husband's side.

I think she really made it a positive experience in her book, but I'm sure there were more downfalls. I'm sure she fought with her husband and was sometimes disappointed to leave each town. But I guess I'll never hear that part of the story.

— 2 —

Harriet Backus had qualities that made her an excellent mining camp wife. While reading Tomboy Bride, *I saw endless examples of this and thoroughly enjoyed these qualities.*

First of all, Harriet was an extremely resourceful woman. She was able to use denim and newspaper for carpet and boxes for furniture. When money was tight, she took the initiative and wrote to a company about improvements George made on their machine. George often had guests over for dinner, and Harriet could always prepare a feast in the small cabin above Telluride. Even if it meant traveling to Mrs. Batcheller's cabin for some canned turkey.

Secondly, Harriet fit into the mining camps well because she was ready to help others. It was her call for help, which enabled men to aid the man and cart dumping tailings. If not for Harriet, they may have gone off the edge. She was there for Mrs. Batcheller when she lost her son Billy. She even helped young Sadie of Elk City in her love pursuits. Harriet arranged for Sadie and her lover to be alone when his stage came.

The most important thing which I think allowed Harriet to make it in the mining camps was her sense of humor and positive outlook. She looks back and laughs at "decayed turkey," "upside down" carmel pie, and bread that never rose. I laughed out loud myself when I read that she accidentally tied young Harriet's bib on George! Although she lost her third child after two days, Harriet remembers her fondly and is thankful for the short time enjoyed with the baby. Harriet doesn't hesitate to go to the shunned "town whore" in Elk City, but even befriends her. She can even laugh in the face of George's broken jaw when describing how silly he looked swollen with bandages and hat.

Overall, we see that Harriet was a witty, resourceful, good neighbor. She had a wonderful sense of humor and a positive attitude that helped her endure the extreme weather and hardships of a mining camp. Not many women could have found so much enjoyment in a world with so few comforts and conveniences.

— 3 —

Harriet Backus was an excellent camping wife with the following qualities about her. She was a supportive, understanding, loving, adventurous, faithful, and courageous person to her husband. The main theme of her qualities is the love for her husband. Because she loved her husband dearly, and family was important, she traveled with her husband through good and bad times.

Harriet Backus was an interesting woman who was tough, not physically but spiritually and emotionally. With these qualities, she endured the different weather, climate and land that she traveled. For example, living in Telluride at the Tomboy Mine, she was snowed in many times. Also, she traveled through snow blizzards to get goods or to go into towns. But Harriet was always by her husband.

Harriet Backus was, overall, an adventurous person who did not mind traveling to isolated areas as long as she was with her loved one, her husband. She is an individual with good qualities such as being sup-

portive, understanding, and loving to her husband.
With these qualities, she did not mind where they were
located or lived as long as she was with her husband.

Harriet Backus was not afraid of hard work, sac-
rifice, adverse conditions and adventures. She was
brave and stoical, and deeply committed to her
beloved husband, George. She was also highly intel-
ligent, inquisitive, and fascinated by anything new.
Most of all she, like her husband (who, in fact,
shared all of these same characteristics) loved every-
thing about nature, which gave her great joy
throughout all of her hardships.

She and George shared everything — his work,
which made her a particularly understanding spouse,
the work and always their love of nature — the beau-
tiful mountains, forests, valleys wherever they lived
— and she must have been a wonderful devoted, and
uplifting wife, friend, mother & neighbor.

— 4 —

Harriet Backus was an excellent mining camp wife
for many reasons. She lived in a world where most
men today couldn't survive. Her first stay in
Telluride away from her home for the first time. The
winters she had to endure. Not knowing how to
order food, to be able to adjust to the altitude and
cook with the little supplies she was able to get from
the mules/pack trains. Just the life style, living in cab-
ins maybe suitable for livestock today.

She was willing to do whatever was necessary to
make things okay. Staying up with the kids or
George all night when they were sick, moving from
Telluride to B.C. to Elk City then to Leadville wher-
ever work was available for her husband.

The time when they were riding back to Tomboy through the snow storm. She continued to go past the Elephant even though she was scared to death. She never complained or the first time she was brought into the mine, climbing the ladder and going deep into the mine — she wanted to know and understand more about her husband's job.

It became very much a part of her life, to endure what she had to put up with shows what a remarkable lady she really was. It's a tough lifestyle which is not for everyone, but once it's in your blood you can't live without it.

She always invited people over for dinner, knowing they would love a home cooked meal. She was a very supportive wife who carried the groceries over her shoulder while pushing Harriet in her cart in four feet of snow. She took care of her part and didn't just rely on her husband.

— 5 —

Harriet Backus was an excellent mining camp wife for many reasons. She probably would have been an excellent wife to any man with any occupation! She was a very strong-willed woman, not afraid to face a challenge, or deal with difficult situations. I don't know too many people that would live at 11,500 feet outside of Telluride even today. Doing it almost one hundred years ago would have been a real challenge. Harriet had no problem although, and even enjoyed her life in the high mountains. She was not afraid to stay alone while George worked or traveled. She always worked very hard around the house and with their daughter. The snow never stopped her, even if it was to deliver a pie to a friend.

She was always willing to go and see where her husband worked, even if it scared her to death! She gave her husband so much support in all that he did. I think one thing that made her and her husband so strong was their love for each other. It was men-tioned several *times throughout the book. She had always said, she could be happy anywhere as long as she was with her love, her husband.*

Overall, she was one of the most strong-willed, fascinating women I have ever read about. She made life good and happy no matter what the circum-stances. She helped George and Harriet through their illnesses (or accidents at the mill, like when George broke his jaw bone badly). She was a wonderful mother of eventually two, a son and a daughter and would have been three, but the second daughter died after two short days of life. Most of all, she was a wonderful wife to her husband.

— 6 —

Marriage is a whole new world. Just married myself I really related to Harriet. She was an amazing woman & very encouraging to me. What made her such an excellent mining camp wife was her willing-ness to be one. She left her home in Oakland, California to be married to George and wanted to experience the mining life and its advantages. Harriet wanted to learn how to be a miner's wife. She had no idea of what to expect so once she reached Telluride, she and George rode the terrifying and long ride to the Tomboy Mine. She never was negative towards her husband from the beginning. She also went wher-ever George was relocated after the Tomboy mine.

Harriet also was devoted to the other women of the mining camps, always giving to them, especially her devotion to her best friend Beth. Harriet also adjusted to the harsh winters and was always willing to trek out in to the snow for the necessities she and George needed. She was a good housekeeper and worked with all she had, she was never discouraged. She struggled with the cooking, but it never got her down. She just tried to improve it the next time.

She was also very loving & supportive and raised a daughter during her husband's mining days. To me that is amazing. Harriet could conquer any storm it seemed. She always looked on the bright side of things. She was thankful for the places & experiences she encountered even when things went wrong at the mill or to her friends or even her loved ones. She was a great mining wife, a really neat lady to read about.

One student summarized Harriet in this manner. "She really does represent a wonderful companion and with all of her excellent qualities, George was a very lucky man. He probably wouldn't have made it in that rough time without his wonderful wife."

As might be imagined, the number of students discussing Harriet came out four to five times more then those who selected George. This was true among both women and men. Here are a couple of samples of their responses to George.

George seemed to be the ideal mining camp husband for many reasons. First of all, he was a dedicated miner and worker. I found it very interesting that despite many hardships such as living conditions, inclement weather, and lack of many necessities, George always managed to make it to work without complaint. However, more dedication was required to being a devoted husband. He always encouraged and praised his wife Harriet to do the best she could. He ensured that Harriet was always able to get supplies of food and coal when it was available. His daily routine of bringing home water after a long day's work proves that he was devoted to his wife and home. This was a difficult task and he never complained. George made their tiny home as comfortable as possible.

He labored continuously shoveling snow to provide access to the outhouse and tried endlessly to remove pack rats from their home. These were very tough times and as a husband and father myself, I hold a lot of respect for George and Harriet for making the best of the worst.

Another agreed with this assessment and added.

George Backus was an excellent mining camp husband. He was a great husband because he shared his love for mining with his wife. When he broke his jaw in Leadville and spent weeks in the hospital, Harriet said that she didn't hear him complain once! I am sure he was in a lot of pain but he didn't want to scare his wife. Plus, he wanted to get back to work and I am sure that Harriet would not have let him go if he was complaining about the pain of his broken jaw.

Finally, he followed his dreams, found a woman that he loved (and that loved him back), worked at a job that he was passionate about and took care of his family. His family was one of the luckiest because he was an excellent mining husband, focused and driven.

It would seem that George and Harriet could not ask for no better legacy then the image these students had of them. *Tomboy Bride* opened the past to show my students the way to move ahead into the future. Harriet, without question, would have approved.

Index